COMPUTER SCIENCE, TECHNOLOGY AND APPLICATIONS

CYBERCULTURE AND THE POTENTIAL EFFECTS ON PERSONNEL SECURITY AND EMPLOYEE PERFORMANCE

COMPUTER SCIENCE, TECHNOLOGY AND APPLICATIONS

Additional books in this series can be found on Nova's website under the Series tab.

Additional e-books in this series can be found on Nova's website under the e-book tab.

COMPUTER SCIENCE, TECHNOLOGY AND APPLICATIONS

CYBERCULTURE AND THE POTENTIAL EFFECTS ON PERSONNEL SECURITY AND EMPLOYEE PERFORMANCE

WALTER P. BARNES
EDITOR

nova publishers
New York

For permission to use material from this book please contact us:
Telephone 631-231-7269; Fax 631-231-8175
Web Site: http://www.novapublishers.com

Library of Congress Cataloging-in-Publication Data

ISBN: 978-1-63117-964-8

Published by Nova Science Publishers, Inc. † New York

CONTENTS

PREFACE

This book provides context, outlines presently actionable findings and strategies, highlights some questions that cannot yet be answered, and draws on outside research to guide future research. It also presents an ethnographic analysis of a popular virtual social environment, Second Life, as the second part of a larger effort to study the impact of involvement in cyberculture on personnel security and safety outcomes.

Chapter 1 – Computers and related technologies, such as smart phones and video games, are now a common part of everyday life. Many people spend a large portion of their waking hours using and socializing through these devices, forming what is known as a cyberculture. Personnel security investigative and adjudicative standards were developed before these products were widely available; however, cyberculture bears relevance to personnel security due both to the presence of existing security issues and potential effects on psychological outcomes and workplace performance. Although cyberculture has many beneficial effects, this project evaluates how participation can negatively affect personnel security and employee performance. This initial report provides context, outlines presently actionable findings and strategies, highlights some questions that cannot yet be answered, and draws on outside research to guide future research. Information from many sources was examined, including academic research journals, other federal organizations, news reports, and cyber environments, to understand cyber activities relevant to personnel security. Participation is widespread in U.S. society and popular among all age groups. Some cyber activities, such as foreign associations, can be reportable per existing investigative criteria, so procedures should be updated appropriately and promptly. Other topics require research before action is recommended. One concern is how online disinhibition, where people who become more willing to disclose personal information, deceive, or become hostile, affects personnel security. Increased willingness to disclose may amplify the counterintelligence concerns for individuals targeted by hostile parties. There are also many potential negative effects on impulse control, mental health, physical health, and workplace behavior. Future research is intended to further guide policy, workforce awareness, investigations, and adjudications.

Chapter 2 – This report presents the results from an ethnographic examination of a popular virtual social environment, Second Life, as the second part of a larger effort to study the impact of participation in cyber activities on personnel security and safety. Research has shown that cyber participation can spill over into individuals' offline lives, which could be of security concern to the extent that their online behavior demonstrates poor judgment and/or undermines their reliability. Several immersive ethnographic methods were used in the present study, including participation observation, group discussions, and one-on-one interviews with 148 Second Life users who resembled the demographics of clearance holders. The reported findings include a description of behaviors of potential concern, a set of case studies that outline the behaviors of actual users, and a framework of user personas that attempts to distinguish between innocuous use of no apparent security concern from problematic use that may pose risks to national security. These findings contain implications for updating personnel security policy regarding cyber involvement.

In: Cyberculture and the Potential Effects ... ISBN: 978-1-63117-964-8
Editor: Walter P. Barnes

Chapter 1

CYBERCULTURE AND PERSONNEL SECURITY: REPORT I – ORIENTATION, CONCERNS, AND NEEDS*

John S. Leggitt, Olga G. Shechter and Eric L. Lang

BACKGROUND

Computers and related technologies, such as smart phones and video games, are now a common part of everyday life. Many people spend a large portion of their waking hours using and socializing through these devices, forming what is known as a cyberculture. Personnel security investigative and adjudicative standards were developed before these products were widely available; however, cyberculture bears relevance to personnel security due both to the presence of existing security issues and potential effects on psychological outcomes and workplace performance. Although cyberculture has many beneficial effects, this project evaluates how participation can negatively affect personnel security and employee performance. This initial report provides context, outlines presently actionable findings and strategies, highlights some questions that cannot yet be answered, and draws on outside research to guide future research.

---

* This is an edited, reformatted and augmented version of Technical Report 11-01, issued by The Defense Personnel and Security Research Center (PERSEREC), dated May 2011.

ABSTRACT

Computers and related technologies, such as smart phones and video games, are now a common part of everyday life. Many people spend a large portion of their waking hours using and socializing through these devices, forming what is known as a cyberculture. Personnel security investigative and adjudicative standards were developed before these products were widely available; however, cyberculture bears relevance to personnel security due both to the presence of existing security issues and potential effects on psychological outcomes and workplace performance. Although cyberculture has many beneficial effects, this project evaluates how participation can negatively affect personnel security and employee performance. This initial report provides context, outlines presently actionable findings and strategies, highlights some questions that cannot yet be answered, and draws on outside research to guide future research. Information from many sources was examined, including academic research journals, other federal organizations, news reports, and cyber environments, to understand cyber activities relevant to personnel security. Participation is widespread in U.S. society and popular among all age groups. Some cyber activities, such as foreign associations, can be reportable per existing investigative criteria, so procedures should be updated appropriately and promptly. Other topics require research before action is recommended. One concern is how online disinhibition, where people who become more willing to disclose personal information, deceive, or become hostile, affects personnel security. Increased willingness to disclose may amplify the counterintelligence concerns for individuals targeted by hostile parties. There are also many potential negative effects on impulse control, mental health, physical health, and workplace behavior. Future research is intended to further guide policy, workforce awareness, investigations, and adjudications.

EXECUTIVE SUMMARY

This report is the first in a planned, ongoing series of studies on how computer technology affects society and psychological outcomes, and in turn, requires changes to personnel security policies and practices. Computers and related products, such as smartphones and portable music players, have become common and many people build their lives around them. In doing so, users have formed cybercultures, or societies that depend on computer technology. These can penetrate broadly and deeply into users' lives, be it through social networks (e.g., Facebook, LinkedIn), online multiplayer games (e.g., World of Warcraft, Call of Duty), virtual social environments (e.g., Second Life, IMVU.com), or other products. Social networks change lives by facilitating communication and planning among friends, family, and associates. Online multiplayer games attract users who spend many hours per day, or entire weekends, to interact, compete, and explore. Virtual social environments, such as Second Life, stand out for enabling a wide range of activities among people from across the world. Finally, mobile devices (e.g., smartphones, iPad) allow unique and perhaps deeper changes due to constant access to the Internet and features such as the ability to track physical movement.

While computer technology has had many positive cultural benefits, such as reducing the costs of obtaining information and helping individuals communicate more effectively, the present research is concerned with negative effects relevant to personnel security. The social and psychological impact of computers represents just a portion of the many cybersecurity concerns facing government and industry. Federal cybersecurity interests range from cyber crime, cyber counterintelligence, and cyber terrorism to many additional concerns that fall under the purview of other federal entities. The present project acknowledges these needs, but directs research efforts only to how psychological and cultural changes impact personnel security. Additional information on the general federal cybersecurity context is available through sources such as the President's Comprehensive National Cybersecurity Initiative (CNCI) and documentation of the diverse cyber activities conducted by the Federal Bureau of Investigation (FBI).

It is also well understood that participation in cyber communities can have numerous individual benefits for education, business, entertainment, shopping, social contact, and more. However, this project is concerned with the potential for serious negative effects and spillover into real life. The present report, as the first in the series, outlines the reasons for concern and presents examples of the concerns, provides immediately actionable strategies for managing known risks, reviews relevant scientific literature, and describes topics requiring future research. Cyber activities potentially affect personnel security practices in two main ways: (1) by creating new venues for generating potential problems, such as making it easier for people to cultivate relationships with foreign nationals or engage in illegal activities, and (2) by transforming conventional methods of interpersonal interaction, such that traditional norms and standards used to assess stability, discretion, and judgment are affected.

In general, those cyber activities involving the migration of known issues to new venues present relatively modest cause for deliberation; rather, modernization requires straightforward updates to clarify reporting requirements, investigator training, and adjudicative guidance. In contrast, research is required for topics that have no precise parallels in traditional society. For example, some people now spend many hours per day interacting through computers and text messaging—to the point of being dependent or perhaps addicted—and this may lead them to share information in a fashion that suggests a lack of discretion. Subsequently, the present report is divided into two parts: (1) Orientation and Actionable Strategies, and (2) Scientific Context and Research Guidance. Part I is meant to lay the groundwork for all readers and sketch ways to move forward, while Part II is intended for those who wish to consider the unknowns in detail or plan specific research projects. Later studies seek to provide concrete recommendations in response to important unanswered questions.

Part I: Orientation and Actionable Strategies

Cyberculture affects several assumptions about human behavior that are presently made during the personnel security vetting process for what is considered normal, responsible, and even knowable. Specifically, it:

1) Often allows for anonymous or depersonalized contact that may dissolve traditional norms and inhibitions.
2) Eliminates the need for geographical proximity, allowing for the easy development of relationships across the world.
3) Expands the potential for blackmail and exploitation by eliminating the real-world costs and consequences of participation, as users who expect complete anonymity can engage in simulated taboo activities they might not otherwise consider.
4) Promotes openness to conversation and sharing personal information as many users join to find chat partners, explore new places, and meet new people.
5) Offers practically unlimited opportunities for willing conversation and activity partners, so vulnerable or isolated people may find it difficult to control their impulsive actions and stop participating.

6) Creates and increases opportunities for exploitation through collecting personal information for minute daily activities, even among strangers in public spaces.

People today can choose among numerous computer products and environments, and while often superficially distinct, the needs and goals of human interaction are largely similar across the board. From a personnel security standpoint, it does not matter whether a person has, for example, developed a reputation for hacking or bad business practices in either a social network, a multiplayer game, or in virtual social environment such as Second Life. Because of this, the present report and its immediate follow-up focus on Second Life for research and examples. Second Life is particularly complex and flexible; it allows optional anonymity; and has an established user base. These characteristics were considered desirable for initial research because they permit efficient coverage of the widest range of cyber behaviors of potential security concern. Many cyber activities duplicate behaviors covered by the Adjudicative Guidelines. For example, virtual interaction with foreign nationals relates to Foreign Influence and Foreign Preference concerns, while participation in fantasy sex (e.g., virtual affairs, orgies, rape, or slavery) could be a Sexual Behavior issue if resulting in secretive behaviors that create avenues for blackmail.

Several actionable strategies about the appropriate personnel security response to cyberculture are immediately possible. These include:

1) Action should be taken to increase awareness across the personnel security community that cyber activities can be functionally identical to real world activities and can present similar risks. Cyber activities that are reportable per the current Adjudicative Guidelines should be explicitly considered along with real world activities.
2) All established cybersecurity topics, such as cyber money laundering, hacking, gang activity, and organized crime, should be systematically reviewed to update personnel security reporting and evaluation guidance.
3) No policy, reporting, or enforcement changes should be made to address novel cyber activities that do not derive directly from existing real-world personnel security standards, unless the changes are supported by empirical evidence.

4) Personnel security policymakers should address how best to evaluate and manage participation in cyber environments. The core needs are to:
   a) Define new and unique cyber topics of potential personnel security interest. Part II presents a range of topics for consideration, and is meant to guide research for this need.
   b) Determine the costs and benefits associated with enacting rules to address new topics.

Readers should also consider the findings of an independent PERSEREC research project that seeks to determine appropriate policies and practices for reviewing online activities, or cybervetting. The cybervetting project emphasizes the requirements for and process of collecting information, rather than the present goal of assessing whether given behaviors are of concern. This program contributed to a report released by the International Association of Chiefs of Police (IACP, 2010) that is meant to guide the law enforcement community. Additionally, work is in progress to adapt the findings for national security positions.

Part II: Scientific Context and Research Guidance

The second part of the report reviews a range of academic research on how computers and related technologies affect psychological outcomes, and presents examples relevant to personnel security. Prior research suggests at least two major reasons for how computer-mediated relationships affect society, including: (1) online disinhibition – where having technological devices eliminates many cues of face-to-face interaction and can result in exaggerated emotions or behaviors, unrealistic expectations, and a lack of perspective, and (2) impulse control problems or cyber addiction – where technology makes social interaction, games, and other preoccupations constantly available such that they negatively impact real world lives. However, data relevant to personnel security are not available, so these preliminary observations do not yet support changes to policies and practices.

Research on the mental health, physical health, and workplace outcomes of problematic computer use is also reviewed to highlight how maladaptive involvement in cyberculture may affect judgment, reliability, and trustworthiness. Mental health research indicates that maladaptive cyber use is associated with a wide range of emotional problems, such as loneliness, low self-esteem, and withdrawal from family activities. Physical health research indicates that excessive cyber use is associated with loss of sleep (and subsequent performance problems the following day), poor nutrition, and a lack of exercise. Excessive use has even resulted in a number of deaths. Finally, trustworthiness and reliability in the workplace can be affected through lying, rule breaking, and circumventing software that blocks access through personal devices. There have also been a number of cases where government employees, including those with high-level security clearances, have accessed pornography at the workplace. In conjunction, these effects might undermine productivity, expose employers to legal liability, create avenues for blackmail, and negatively impact rules put in place to protect sensitive or classified information.

In looking toward the future, this report sketches research now in progress, specific plans, and other research needs. Report II, as completed in parallel with Report I, examines activities in Second Life in context of the potentially disqualifying behaviors specified in the Adjudicative Guidelines. This study focuses on users who resemble personnel security clearance holders, including being U.S. citizens, holding jobs, and those willing to undergo employment-related background screening. Future research is to use quantitative survey methods to assess the likely prevalence rates of behaviors of concern in a diverse range of cyber environments among individuals who resemble clearance holders and applicants, and also to generate actionable recommendations for investigations, adjudications, and workplace management. Finally, mobile computers and pervasive computing devices (e.g., those in vehicles, embedded in other equipment, or situated in public locations) present unique risks and should receive focused attention.

INTRODUCTION

Background and Problem

Computer technology has spread throughout modern society and is often an integral part of everyday life. It facilitates a wide range of necessary and popular activities, such as communication, shopping, finance, news, education, research, games, hobbies, and socializing—and the time people spend using computing devices is increasing. For example, the Kaiser Family Foundation estimates that young people now use entertainment media devices 53 hours a week, which amounts to 7 hours and 38 minutes per day (Rideout, Foehr, &

Roberts, 2010). Similarly, a May, 2010 telephone survey found that 40% of those over the age of 50 are very or extremely comfortable using the Internet, and 27% of those over 50 accesses social media sites such as Facebook (AARP, 2010). The present research examines the personnel security implications of a society, or a cyberculture, dependent on computers.

The American Heritage Dictionary of the English Language (2010) defines cyberculture as "The culture arising from the use of computer networks, as for communication, entertainment, work, and business." Cyberculture has a strong presence in the federal workplace, through the widespread use of personal computers, BlackBerry products, and other devices, and the apparent trend is toward even greater use. For example, the Virtual Government (vGov) initiative of the National Defense University, U.S. Air Force, Homeland Security Department, and Agriculture Department seeks to facilitate collaboration and virtual meetings in the immersive environment of virtual worlds (Lipowicz, 2010). Cyberculture, however, has also drawn personnel security attention and resulted in new personnel security concerns. In April 2009, the Intelligence Advanced Research Projects Activity (IARPA), the research arm of the Office of the Director of National Intelligence (ODNI), unveiled the Reynard Program. Reynard is a multidisciplinary research effort aimed at identifying behavioral indicators in virtual worlds and online multiplayer games that correspond to the real world characteristics of users (Bush, 2009). Similarly, an article in the *Federal Times* warned individuals that their postings and contacts on social networking websites might preclude them from gaining and keeping a security clearance (Rinckey, 2009).

It is crucial to understand that the cultural impact of computers represents only a portion of the many cybersecurity concerns faced by government and industry. The term cybersecurity refers to general security problems associated with computers. Some of the most high-profile federal cybersecurity activities include the President's Comprehensive National Cybersecurity Initiative (CNCI), the 2009 establishment of the Department of Defense U.S. Cyber Command (USCYBERCOM), and a wide range of cyber programs of the Federal Bureau of Investigation (FBI). However, many important questions do not have immediate answers and are reportedly not being presently addressed. A June, 2010 Government Accountability Office (GAO) report states that cybersecurity research is crucial but lacks effective oversight and management, and GAO urges prompt federal action. The report argues that without a broad national cybersecurity agenda, research tends to focus on the short term and the needs of individual stakeholders, rather than what may be most important from a national perspective. The present research and other federal actions should be viewed in this context, where unity and the big picture must be a high priority, but also an environment requiring prompt and targeted responses to obvious needs.

The main points of the CNCI are presented below to illustrate where personnel security and cyberculture fit in the more general cybersecurity context. The CNCI is perhaps the most widely known attempt to summarize the range of needs and risks for economic and national security, "designed to help secure the United States in cyberspace." Some items refer to specific immediate needs (e.g., the deployment of intrusion detection and prevention systems), while others initiatives are open-ended and seemingly in an early stage (e.g., coordinate R&D efforts, define and develop "leap-ahead" activities). Interested parties should refer to the original document for additional details. The three main goals of the CNCI are:

1) To establish a front line of defense against today's immediate threats
2) To defend against the full spectrum of threats
3) To strengthen the future cybersecurity environment

The 12 supporting initiatives are:

1) Manage the Federal Enterprise Network as a single network enterprise with Trusted Internet Connections.
2) Deploy an intrusion detection system of sensors across the Federal enterprise.
3) Pursue deployment of intrusion prevention systems across the Federal enterprise.
4) Coordinate and redirect research and development (R&D) efforts.
5) Connect current cyber ops centers to enhance situational awareness.
6) Develop and implement a government-wide cyber counterintelligence (a.k.a. CI) plan.
7) Increase the security of our classified networks.
8) Expand cyber education.
9) Define and develop enduring "leap-ahead" technology, strategies, and programs.
10) Define and develop enduring deterrence strategies and programs.
11) Develop a multi-pronged approach for global supply chain risk management.
12) Define the Federal role for extending cybersecurity into critical infrastructure.

Federal cybersecurity measures move forward at different rates between areas, but the FBI provides many examples of clear and concrete progress. The FBI created a cyber division in 2002, has provided cyber training to thousands of its staff, and has been actively working to reduce the risks of cyber terrorism, cyber espionage and cyber crime. In addition, it disseminated more than 1,800 cyber intelligence and cyber analytic products to the Intelligence Community, military, law enforcement, and Department of Homeland Security in Fiscal Year 2009. There are also said to be counterterrorism and counterintelligence efforts that must be discussed in a secure forum (Chabinsky, 2009). Some of the cyber crimes tackled by the FBI include child pornography and the exploitation of children, Internet fraud, and more (Snow, 2010).

Personnel security emphasizes those threats most closely associated with the actions of the cleared workforce. These can originate externally, as when a spy or hacker actively seeks and gathers information, or from inside, as when a trusted employee becomes careless, disgruntled, has sympathy for a foreign government, or seeks to profit from their knowledge. A wide variety of procedures are employed, including requiring that job applicants undergo background investigations and the monitoring of relevant employee behaviors. All together, this system seeks to distinguish members of the workforce who are able to protect sensitive information from those who pose a security risk. Executive Order (E.O.) 12968 describes this goal by stating that eligibility for access to classified information should be granted only to individuals whose character affirmatively indicates trustworthiness, honesty, reliability, discretion, and sound judgment.

All personal characteristics and activities relevant to the safeguarding of sensitive information are of legitimate interest for national security, and many topics are considered when assessing who is to be entrusted with sensitive information. For example, investigations now consider financial history, criminal records, allegiance to the United States, contact or association with citizens of foreign countries, and much more. The emergence of cyberculture raises a new concern because it affects many previous assumptions about personal behavior, as well as if or how cyber behaviors can be investigated. Unfortunately, it is not clear how some cyber activities might relate to traditional interpretations of reliability, trustworthiness, and good judgment. For example, cyber communities often allow anonymous participation, so it is relatively easy to misrepresent oneself and gain access to those in sensitive positions who might otherwise be on guard for exploitation.

In 2010, a security consultant created a social network profile for a fictitious young, attractive, "foreign looking" woman who identified herself as a "cyber threat analyst" working for the U.S. Navy. Almost 300 people in the military, security, and intelligence communities established connections with her within a month, including those in senior positions and organizations such as the Joint Chiefs of Staff, the National Reconnaissance Office, the U.S. Marine Corps, staff of a U.S. congressperson, and major defense contractors. The fictitious woman received invitations to speak at a conference and review a technical paper, and several invited her to apply for jobs (Waterman, 2010).

The greatest unknown from a personnel security standpoint is the potential impact of life-long cyber socialization, or growing up and predominantly interacting through cyberculture, on overall judgment and behavior in the workplace.

The concern is that some individuals may internalize cyber world norms in a way that compromises their ability to distinguish between cyber and physical world rules for social interaction and the consequences of actions. The ultimate impact cannot be known until the children growing up today have received security clearances and spent significant time in the workforce, but what is presently known about cyber involvement indicates that over the short term it can harm health, be psychologically maladaptive, and have other negative consequences.

Some of the specific problems now observed among cyber participants include patterns of behavior similar to the addictive and compulsive behaviors described in the Diagnostic and Statistical Manual of Mental Disorders, 4t^{h} Ed. (DSM-IV, 1994), and studies report that Internet addicts possess higher levels of depressive symptoms than non-addicts (Morrison & Gore, 2010). Other commonly expressed concerns include social isolation due to reliance on virtual communication, and a lack of discretion in what information is shared with others (e.g., a college student showing pictures of binge drinking episodes on Facebook or a congressman inadvertently disclosing his sensitive whereabouts while traveling through Iraq and Afghanistan [Flaherty, 2009]). Finally, research reviewed in the *Biologist* indicates that increased dependence on technology has negative consequences for sleep, immune system functioning, morbidity, and mortality (Sigman, 2009). In sum, these observations indicate that further study is required, and subsequently the present research project assesses the personnel security implications of widespread cultural reliance on computer technology.

Project Goals

This report is the first in a planned, ongoing series of studies about personnel security concerns associated with participation in cyberculture, focusing on the psychological outcomes and workplace performance relevant to cleared individuals. This project acknowledges but does not emphasize cybersecurity issues resulting from hostile parties, such as espionage or crime, as they are being addressed by other federal entities. Future studies are intended to use empirical methods to build on what has been learned, and provide a deeper understanding than would be possible otherwise.

The present report provides background information on the personnel security relevance of cyberculture, as based on reviews of academic literature, media reports, websites, and a variety of cyber environments. It introduces core issues, highlights what can be determined immediately, and outlines examples of topics requiring future research. The document is divided into two parts:

1) **Orientation and Actionable Strategies:** An overview of how and why cyberculture impacts personnel security, with the goal of assisting personnel security community stakeholders in moving forward rapidly and efficiently. Several examples are used to illustrate immediate points of action.
2) **Scientific Context and Research Guidance:** Material of particular interest to those who seek awareness or who are planning for the future, such as for designing or funding research projects and policy working groups. Examples of a diverse array of cyberculture topics illustrate potential concerns that are not presently actionable.

Cyberculture Research Program

Additional research is presently in progress or has already been completed. A second study, "Cyber Culture and Personnel Security: Report II - Ethnographic Analysis of Second Life," was conducted in parallel with the present research. It explored potentially problematic behavior patterns that occur in a cyber world. Using qualitative ethnographic research methods, users who chose to participate and who resemble clearance holders (e.g., those who are employed or looking for work, have held, currently hold, or would consider a job requiring a background investigation, are U.S. citizens, etc.) were observed and interviewed. The participants' cyber behaviors were analyzed in the context of the Adjudicative Guidelines, and an initial framework for understanding behaviors of potential personnel security concern was generated.

Research now in progress seeks to use quantitative methods to assess the prevalence rates for cyber activities of potential concern and generate recommendations for policy and best practices. This is intended to be useful for all personnel security stakeholders, including the cleared workforce, policymakers, investigators, adjudicators, and field management. Additional studies are to be initiated as appropriate.

Other PERSEREC Cyber Research

An independent PERSEREC project seeks to generate appropriate policies and practices for reviewing online activities, or cybervetting. While the (present) cyberculture project studies *behaviors* of apparent personnel security concern, the cybervetting project addresses the legal and technical requirements for, and process of collecting, information to satisfy investigative coverage requirements. The cybervetting project contributed to a report released by the International Association of Chiefs of Police (IACP, 2010) that is meant to guide vetting in the law enforcement community. Additionally, work is in progress to adapt the findings for national security positions.

PART I: ORIENTATION AND ACTIONABLE STRATEGIES

An Increasingly Computerized Culture

Computer technology has so many uses and so much flexibility that it regularly changes how people perform common activities. Many of these changes affect how people go about their business, but are ultimately unremarkable from a personnel security perspective. Examples include using email instead of a telephone, using online banking instead of sending checks through the mail, looking up information on the web instead of using an encyclopedia or a telephone book, and comparison shopping through a website rather than with catalogs or by visiting local stores. Instead, the important questions are if and how dependence on computer technology might affect thinking and socialization, whereby presently accepted personnel security standards no longer effectively differentiate between behaviors that pose a risk to controlled information, nor between reliable and unreliable employees. People who grow up and spend the bulk of their waking hours surrounded by such technology may conduct their personal lives in different ways, may behave differently in the workplace, and take a different approach to tasks or respond differently to direction from management.

Society seemingly changes in conjunction with computer technologies. A New York Times story argues that technological generation gaps are now occurring at a rapid pace, such that there are differences in the cyber activities of young children, those in their teens, their twenties, their thirties, and older (Stone, 2010). A Computerworld.com essay notes that those currently between the ages of 20 and 60 are the only people in human history to communicate with traditional one-to-one (e.g., letters, telephone) and one-to-many (e.g., radio, newspaper, television) methods, as well as the new any-to-any method of social networking (Elgan, 2010). Subrahmanyam and Greenfield (2008) outline how adolescents growing up today face a broad array of new technologies, and that many basic questions have not been studied. They also point out that contemporary social networking applications have made conclusions about the Internet from just 10 or 15 years ago obsolete. Subsequently, to understand technologies with the greatest potential for affecting cognition, socialization, and workplace behavior, the present research seeks those involving the greatest changes relative to noncomputerized cultures.

Three current implementations of cyberculture stand out as being widespread and popular, having participants who display strong and persistent interest, and for providing ways to substantially change social, hobby, and other aspects of personal lives. They include: (1) social networks (e.g., Facebook, MySpace), (2) online multiplayer games (e.g., World of Warcraft, Everquest), and (3) virtual social environments (e.g., Second Life, IMVU). These are now common across American society, and adults frequently participate, rather than just teenagers and college students. Social network participation is expanding in all age groups. For example, a *2010 Facebook Demographics and Statistics Report* showed that approximately two thirds of all Facebook users were adults 25 and older (Corbett, 2010). The fastest growing Facebook demographics were adults 35-54 years old and adults aged 55+. The 35-54 demographic grew by 25.2% between January and June 2010, while the 55+ demographic grew 35.3% in the same period. An August 2010 report (Pew Research Center) indicates that social networking among those over 50 years of age increased from 22% to 42% in the prior year, and 26% of those over 65 now use social networks. Similarly, video games are estimated to be played in 65% of American households and the average gamer is now 35 years old (Weaver et al., 2009). Statistics reported by Linden Lab in 2008 show that 84% of Second Life users are 25 and older, and that adults aged 25-

34 make-up the largest demographic of all Second Life users (34%). Each type is briefly introduced below, and then they are discussed together to highlight universal commonalities. Finally, all cyber activities are affected by mobile devices with unique security concerns, and mobile technology itself has the potential to more thoroughly change society.

Social Networks

In the simplest sense, an online social network provides an efficient way of sharing and obtaining personal information. Some of the most widely known and popular social networks include Facebook, MySpace, and LinkedIn. They have become a common method for maintaining social contact with friends and family, as well as for finding employment and other individuals with similar interests. The Nielsen Report (2010) states that three fourths of those who go online across the world now use social media websites (which also include blogs, Wikipedia, and YouTube), that 22% of all time spent online occurs at these sites, and that usage has been rapidly increasing. Social networks typically combine general information about a person, the ability to send messages, immediate updates on current activities, and a way of organizing topic-specific interests, photographs, hobbies, or games. They represent a significant shift from previous methods of social contact by efficiently bringing together a wide range of people and personal information in one place. As the information in social networks is primarily about real people, the main decisions facing users are whether to share the information at all, and how to control the information available to each circle of associates (e.g., family vs. business associates vs. friends).

Social networks raise concerns for employers because potential or current employees can exercise poor judgment with the activities, associates, and information they share about themselves. The longer-term question is how social networks might affect cultural standards for privacy. An Internet security firm surveyed 2,200 mothers across 10 industrialized countries with Internet access and children aged 2 or younger. They found that the average child acquires an online presence at 6 months and 81% have a digital footprint (e.g., photos, pre-birth scans, email addresses, etc.) by age 2 (Smith, J., 2010). Furthermore, the author argues that people under 20 years of age now naturally share information through Facebook, as for them it resembles chatting at the water cooler with colleagues, so it must eventually be permitted in the workplace. In addition, the founder and CEO of Facebook, Mark Zuckerberg, has made several highly controversial statements and management decisions on privacy, such as saying that people now care less about keeping information private than previous generations (Kirkpatrick, 2010).

To the extent that society is changing in the direction of sharing more information, social networks may present additional challenges for the protection of private, proprietary, and classified information. The consequences of sharing are potentially much more damaging than in the past, for material can now be immediately transmitted across the world and stored indefinitely. As described in the introduction, a security consultant demonstrated that many personnel security professionals quickly befriended an attractive but fraudulent peer on social networks (Waterman, 2010). Similarly, Facebook progressively relaxed its default privacy settings over the last several years, moving from sharing only with friends, schools, and personal networks to now sharing almost all information with anyone across the Internet (McKeon, 2010). To illustrate how such data might be exploited, another security consultant used software to read and compile the public information of 171 million Facebook users (one third of the 2010 total of 500 million), and made it available for downloading (Paul, 2010).

Online Multiplayer Games

Online multiplayer games, which are played through a wide variety of computer and video game devices (e.g., desktops, notebooks, Playstation, Xbox, iPhone, etc.), provide a way of matching people for competition, social interaction, group participation, or cooperation to achieve a common objective. Multiplayer games can be as basic as finding a partner for checkers, or involve thousands of simultaneous players in near photorealistic virtual environments that simulate a city, kingdom, racetrack, battlefield, etc. Many popular games (e.g., Call of Duty, Halo, Quake, Doom, etc.) focus on virtual armed combat between individuals or groups. In addition, online games often incorporate complex stories that parallel an epic film or lengthy novel, and use a form of social networking through guilds or teams (e.g., World of Warcraft, Everquest, etc.).

While computer and video games have often been criticized for promoting or desensitizing users to violence (Carnagey, Anderson, & Bushman, 2007; Dill & Dill, 1998), they also have military purposes. For example, since 2002, the U.S. Department of Defense (DoD) has been using a game called America's Army as a recruitment and training tool (White, 2005; AmericasArmy.com, 2010). Similarly, pilots stationed near Las Vegas use a computerized remote control system that strongly resembles flight simulator games to fly unmanned aircraft over Afghanistan and Iraq that fire real weapons and result in real deaths (Frontline, 2009). These examples show that game technology clearly has useful roles in the military, so the functional benefits of games must be distinguished from any unwanted negative effects.

Of the greatest interest for the present research, online multiplayer games change traditional society by eliminating many real world limitations characteristic of competition and team interaction. For example, before computers were available, an individual desiring competition might have visited a community center, organized a poker game, played chess by mail, or joined a local baseball league. Today, however, a person can find instant matches through thousands of products and with millions of players. Competitors can be found any time of the day, during bad weather, and when no one nearby shares similar interests. The most apparent security-relevant consequence is that the all-you-can-eat atmosphere may promote acting on impulse or result in clinical addiction among susceptible individuals. Research indicates that some game designs are consistent with a reward system that promotes greater and longer use, as developers profit through ongoing user subscriptions (Ducheneaut, Yee, Nickell, & Moore, 2006). Furthermore, the social components of online multiplayer games parallel social networks, and social networks also include games (e.g., FarmVille, CityVille, Café World, FrontierVille, Mafia Wars, etc.). As socially networked games tend to be more popular among female players and those outside the 18-34 age group, they expand the concerns for personnel security and the workplace beyond those traditionally recognized for young males who play games (Gross, 2010).

Virtual Social Environments

A 3D virtual environment is a simulated physical place, be it real or imaginary, created through computers. A user or users can "be" in that place through a computer display, most often using a first-person "through the eyes" or a third-person "over the shoulder" view. Many games employ virtual environments, but virtual environments have other purposes too. Second Life is probably the most well known virtual social environment, and it has a much broader scope than any game. It was released by Linden Lab in 2003 and has experienced many changes over subsequent years (Clark, 2010). While it visually resembles a game, it is meant to provide a way of sharing user-created content, locations, and experiences rather than be a game per se. Users choose what to do and can buy virtual real estate to build what they wish, so, due to this flexibility, it may exhibit the widest range of activities of any virtual environment. Within this flexible design, it shares many aspects of both social networks and multiplayer games. Going beyond games, Second Life users have no explicit goals, but they can play games if desired. Going beyond social networks, Second Life users need not share their name but can choose to reveal their identity and interests, as well as maintain a list of associates.

Between 2005 and 2008, Second Life received widespread media attention and experienced rapid changes due to well-funded experimentation by businesses, individuals, and organizations who perceived it as an opportunity for being at the forefront of the cultural changes enabled by computer networks. As described below, news stories from that era discuss Second Life's growing popularity, all that was attempted with the minimal restrictions Linden Lab placed on virtual real estate, and the things that failed. The optimism associated with trying new ideas led to a rushed atmosphere and generous spending relative to the rewards, much like the 1990s-2000s dot-com, real estate, and financial bubbles. An influential magazine cover story described how a single person owned virtual real estate worth $250,000 U.S., and made money from virtual rentals and sales (Businessweek, 2006). Corporations including Best Buy, Cisco, Reuters, Pontiac, Dell, H&R Block, and more created elaborate in-world locations (Brandon, 2007), but interest quickly declined because users simply did not visit corporate sites (Semuels, 2007). In-world banking and gambling also rose in popularity, but were then banned by Linden Lab due to various difficulties and real-world laws (Reuters, 2007; Terdiman, 2008). IBM pushed for the use of virtual worlds in corporate environments, such as remote meetings and conferences (Brodkin, 2008). Finally, as early as 2007, more than 300 real-world universities established a presence in Second Life, and used it for remote teaching and course supplementation (Sussman, 2007); however, educational institution interest may now have shifted or expanded to other virtual worlds (Young, 2010).

In the aftermath of the publicity and many failed attempts at commercialization, Second Life now has a lower profile but apparently a strong business niche. Statistics show that usage is increasing and is at an all time high, with 826,214 monthly unique logins for repeat visitors as of March 2010 (Nino, 2010; Hopkins, 2010). Similarly, user-to-user financial transactions for 2009 were worth $567 million U.S. (Rosenwald, 2010) and $160 million U.S. in the first quarter of 2010, which are also all time highs (Hopkins, 2010). Although Linden Lab announced some layoffs in 2010 associated with consolidation efforts (Woollacott, 2010), virtual social environments such as Second Life are likely to be popular for the foreseeable future. Examples from Second Life are used throughout the present report because it makes a wide range of activities possible, and because the second report on cyberculture focused on its users.

Common Characteristics of Popular Cyber Environments

Different cyber environments often provide similar experiences to their users, as all of them facilitate social activities through computer technology rather than face-to-face interaction. The examples presented above are merely snapshots, for there is no single version of cyberculture and each implementation constantly changes. In fact, many environments are tending to adopt the features and capabilities of each other and become ever more similar in the process.

In many ways it is pointless to draw clear lines between social networks, multiplayer online games, and virtual social environments. Facebook games such as FarmVille, CityVille, and Mafia Wars give players an advantage for linking to friends who also play, and linking is necessary for advancement (Chen, 2009; Gross, 2010; Mafiawarstips.com, 2010). World of Warcraft players must eventually join social guilds or teams to complete difficult challenges and make progress in the game (Ducheneaut, et al., 2006), and the CEO of Activision Publishing said that the online game Call of Duty "has in many ways become one of the world's most engaged social networks" (Albanesius, 2010).

Apple announced a social network for game players, whereby users of their smartphones can find opponents, collect achievements, and see competitive rankings on scoreboards (Steinberg, 2010). Finally, Linden Lab plans to move Second Life to web browser software, mobile devices, and extend it for integration with social networks such as Facebook (Woollacott, 2010).

Many examples of cyberculture largely overlap, seemingly because activities are popular only when interesting or useful from an ordinary human standpoint. Regardless of technology, people continue to have the same needs and goals in life, including finding companionship, entertainment, or satisfying employment, and building families.

As such, popular cyber environments succeed by touching on these interests and naturally tend to be similar. The characteristics of each type of environment are presented in Table 1 (page 12), and their commonalities are summarized in the remainder of this section. Table 1 also outlines the most apparent potential security risks for each type of cyber environment. For those readers who prefer a narrative description, the captions below the table provide similar information.

Table 1. Comparison between Social Networks, Online Multiplayer Games, and Virtual Social Environments

	Social Networks	**Online Multiplayer Games**	**Virtual Social Environments**
Major Goals	Share personal information, interests, and activities with family, friends, and associates. Also used for games, shopping, advertising, etc.	Compete against or cooperate with others to achieve a common goal, often including a fantasy element; social interaction; buying and selling of game objects.	Social interaction; fantasy and role-play; shopping; virtual art and tourism; games; music; video; design; business meetings; education.
Level of Privacy	Low – the primary purpose is to share real-life information.	High or low – chosen by each user.	High or low – chosen by each user.
Breadth of Activities and Choices Available	High – many users, groups, and activities. Because users' identities are generally known, participation often involves impression management[1] or discretion.	Low to moderate – games are typically designed to have clear competitive objectives, controls to prevent cheating, and ways to manage user interaction.	High – designed for flexibility and comprehensive options, plus optional anonymity eliminates societal barriers to experimentation with alternate lifestyles.
Major Topics of Apparent Relevance to Personnel Security and Real Life Spillover	1. Lack of discretion about the information revealed may reflect poorly on judgment and open the door to identity theft or exploitation. 2. Clinical addiction or impulse control disorders. 3. Easy communication with foreign nationals. 4. Hacking.	1. Clinical addiction or impulse control disorders, amplified by designs whereby developers profit by promoting heavy and long-term use. 2. Activities such as photorealistic simulated violence may blur the fantasy vs. reality boundary. 3. Excessive spending to support a hobby. 4. Easy communication with foreign nationals. 5. Hacking.	1. Lack of discretion coupled with engagement in simulated taboo activities. 2. Clinical addiction or impulse control disorders. 3. Easy communication with foreign nationals. Illegal activities such as gambling or simulated pedophilia. Excessive fantasizing may blur the boundary with reality. 6. Excessive spending to support a hobby. 7. Hacking.

- *Major Goals:* Social interaction is universally popular, and while many environments offer a wide range of activities, each user chooses what to do. Virtual social environments generally offer the widest variety of potential goals and are also the most flexible, as the developer does not dictate users' goals. Note that social networks are rapidly gaining new capabilities too.
- *Level of Privacy:* The main difference among the types is that social networks are designed to share personal information, so users must reveal information to fully and effectively participate, while identity is often a secondary consideration or irrelevant in the other cyber environments.
- *Breadth of Activities and Choices Available:* Online multiplayer games stand out as being more goal-oriented and less flexible than social networks or virtual social environments. Games are designed primarily for competition and achievement whereas social networks and virtual social environments are intended for diverse activities.
- *Major Topics of Apparent Relevance to Personnel Security and Real-Life Spillover:* All three types share the potential for excessive use or spending, hacking, and social engineering or exploitation by hostile parties. In addition:
  1) Social networks, in facilitating real-life relationships, present a particular concern as tools for collecting, organizing, and storing evidence suggesting poor judgment and a lack of discretion. Due to weak privacy restrictions, people can also be victimized by the decisions of associates (e.g., a friend posting detrimental photos), and hostile parties (e.g., foreign governments) might easily profile and target those likely to possess valuable information.
  2) Online multiplayer games usually involve a limited range of competitive goals, but if designed to encourage more and longer play, vulnerable participants may be more likely to experience impulse control problems or become clinically addicted. Games have a strong fantasy component, so certain individuals or heavy users may confuse real life and cyber rules. Note that some social network games inform real-life "friends" of activities that may suggest overuse, and subsequently reveal poor judgment.
  3) Virtual social environments present the broadest range of concerns because of their flexibility. The potential concerns include all those found with social networks and online multiplayer games. However, with optional anonymity, users may

be more open about sharing private information, resulting in greater vulnerabilities if a real identity becomes known.

Living in a Mobile and Pervasive Cyberculture

Cyberculture involves truly conducting one's life through computer technology, and this means that numerous aspects of daily life can be affected. The discussion has considered how cyber activities shape and supplant a wide range of real world activities, but the impact extends well beyond desktop and notebook computers, and beyond sitting passively in chairs. Most notably, people participate through smartphones and pocket computers, but also through pervasive computing devices, such as those encountered in vehicles, appliances, kiosks, televisions, alarm clocks, or anything else with Internet access. In fact, nontraditional computers both duplicate traditional concerns and result in unique security concerns. They more fully illustrate what it really means to live today in a cyberculture.

Having easy and continuous access to computers opens the door to two major outcomes. First, it increases the potential for outright dependence, whereby people literally cannot function without them. In some sense this is obvious and unremarkable, as many professionals today would be unable to function without cell phones or smartphones, but the impact is broadening over time. Dependence is discussed more generally in Part II of the present report, as firm conclusions require further research. Second, mobile computers have the same basic characteristics of all computers, so they "attach" these to each and every daily activity. On the positive side, users gain the power to obtain detailed information about any topic at any time, but on the negative side people carry with them known computer security concerns, including hacking, social engineering, and additional pathways for exploitation. As phones with features such as picture taking, Internet access, email, instant messaging, games, and music are now commonly used by Americans (Smith, A., 2010), such products are of immediate interest.

Mobile and pervasive computing bring traditional security concerns to more and more places in daily life. Location-based services integrate real-world places (i.e., physical locations/GPS coordinates) with Internet information to help users be more knowledgeable and efficient as they move about the world. Some of the more well-known products include Foursquare (social networking, exploration), Gowalla (social networking, exploration), Urbanspoon (restaurant finder), and Yelp (restaurant and business finder, user reviews). While in the past a person looking for a good restaurant might have asked at a hotel or gas station, or simply wandered around looking for a crowd, users today can search the surrounding area for a type of food, for those with the best reviews, or for those open at a given time. These products can be enormously useful, but it is effectively impossible to ensure that the information provided is accurate or being handled ethically. For example, Yelp has been sued for extortion and fraud, with claims that Yelp's sales staff promised to remove negative business reviews only if the businesses paid to advertise. At the time of writing, Yelp has denied the allegations (Ali, 2010). Theoretically, a business such as this might manipulate independent companies, or be a front for a hostile entity that tracks user movement, identifies individuals with valuable information, and facilitates the recruitment of agents.

Additional topics of security interest arise from the information that users share and collect on their own. For example, one's GPS location can be combined with photos taken by a smartphone to obtain information about landmarks of interest to tourists, find the identity of artwork, obtain additional product information in a store (Google, 2010), and even the name and personal details of a stranger who has a photo in the Facebook database (Chang, 2010). As long a photo can be taken and the Internet searched, there is no limit to what a person could learn about those around them. Users could find people who are looking for a partner, are a friend-ofa-friend, share a common hobby, share religious beliefs, share a political ideology, or have other characteristic of interest (Ionescu, 2010). An example of the impact comes from a Twitter user in South Africa who updates 6,000 followers about police roadblocks and speed traps so motorists can avoid fines and delay. While some of his followers view him as a hero, the police considered charging him with obstructing justice (BBC News, 2010). The chief security concern is that, in the process of increasing users capabilities, they also increase the power of other individuals to track and target people for exploitation. In fact, both the U.S. Air Force and U.S. Army have issued warnings about how location sharing can assist hostile forces (Diana, 2010).

Information sharing among mobile device users has transformed how many social and political events are organized, and also how the participants interact with other segments of society. A flash mob is a quickly organized group that meets in a public location for any number of purposes (Kelkar, 2010), but often for performance art or to create a social event. For example, Star Wars fans in England organized one at a shopping mall to conduct a mass light saber fight (Zani, 2010), a group of 70 Ohio State University students started singing and dancing in unison (Henthorn, 2010), and a flash mob snowball fight in Philadelphia ended in vandalism and violence (Sheridan,

2010). Several foreign governments have suppressed information resources to control political opposition, which clearly demonstrates a deep impact. In early 2011, social media were a factor in driving the Tunisian leader from the country, and shortly thereafter political flash mobs were organized to protest the Egyptian government (Timpane, 2011). The Egyptian government responded by cutting off virtually all Internet and mobile communication, and this was much more comprehensive than similar government shutdowns of communication by Iran in 2009 and Myanmar in 2007 (El Gazzar, Vitorovich, & Bender, 2011).

The most important generalization about mobile and pervasive computing is that everyone is affected, regardless of whether one chooses to participate. This is because strangers can access vast information resources and have a far greater impact than in past generations. The ability to learn personal information now extends beyond friends and associates to private businesses, hostile or illegitimate governments, and literally anyone with a mobile device. The mere presence of computing devices in public locations combines all long-established real world security risks with those made possible by the web, and voluntary participants may differ from nonparticipants for expectations of privacy and discretion.

Summary

Cyberculture alters several basic assumptions about human behavior that are presently made during the personnel security vetting process for what is considered normal, responsible, and even knowable. The current investigative standards and Adjudicative Guidelines were developed when cyberculture was restricted to small segments of society and an afterthought. Now that computer-mediated culture has entered the mainstream, regular participation should be expected across the cleared population. The core need going forward is to recognize what stays the same as computers enter the picture versus what changes. In sum, cyberculture:

1) Often allows for anonymous or depersonalized contact that may dissolve traditional norms and inhibitions.
2) Eliminates the need for geographical proximity, allowing for the easy development of relationships across the world.
3) Expands the potential for blackmail and exploitation by eliminating the real-world costs and consequences of participation, as users who expect complete anonymity can engage in simulated taboo activities they might not otherwise consider.

4) Promotes openness to conversation and sharing personal information as many users join to find chat partners, explore new places, and meet new people.
5) Offers practically unlimited opportunities for willing conversation and activity partners, so vulnerable or isolated people may find it difficult to control their impulsive actions and stop participating.
6) Creates and increases opportunities for exploitation through collecting personal information for minute daily activities, even among strangers in public spaces.

Personnel security investigations and workforce management have long considered information from real-world friends, family, and associates, as well as traceable activities maintained by external parties, such as crime reports and financial records. The emergence of cyberculture adds to what may be important to consider, and the inherent differences can require the rethinking of policies or additional research. Some of the resulting questions include:

1) How to determine and evaluate when cyber activities materially and adversely spill over to real-life relationships, attitudes, and practices.
2) Whether background investigations can and should consider fantasy activities that may intentionally blur legal boundaries.
3) Whether any cyber activity performed with a reasonable expectation of anonymity needs to be reported or should be considered.
4) Whether anonymous activities in certain cyber environments can be effectively investigated or confirmed.

None of these questions were answerable on the basis of previous research or accepted standards and practices. Those topics that can be addressed are discussed at the end of Part I, while Part II and planned follow-up research seek to establish more practical and specific recommendations for the personnel security community.

Second Life: One Manifestation of Cyberculture

Overview

People today have millions of cyber communities to choose among. Many are simple and limited, such as special interest blogs or discussion groups (e.g., finance, movies, politics, automobiles, music, etc.) that present news items and allow readers to comment using a real or fictitious screen name, while others impact a broad range of interests and activities. The discussion above outlined a range of complex types, but as can be easily confirmed through first-hand experience, many activities and social patterns tend to be similar across communities. The choice of which community to join, and which ones become enduring and important to a user, depend on factors such as personal hobbies and interests, the desire to explore, the presence of or recruitment by friends and family, news events that have sparked curiosity, and more.

Second Life was selected for initial research because it provides an efficient way to observe many topics relevant to personnel security. A wide range of activities are possible, including classes from real colleges, business meetings, virtual tourism, buying and selling virtual goods, socializing, and special interest clubs; it has a well-established user base, which is beneficial for assessing the long-term impact of participation; its graphics make it possible to visualize the reasons for concern; and its optional anonymity increases the chances of encountering users who experiment with activities that could negatively impact their real lives. Anonymous users, such as people with fictitious social network identities, have no incentive for maintaining a reputation or avoiding activities that would be frowned upon by colleagues, friends, or family. All in all, Second Life provides a good way to illustrate the broad impact of a cyber social hub.

An important question resulting from the choice of Second Life revolves around how typical it is versus other cyber communities. As discussed above, the complexity, fluidity, and diversity of modern products largely prevent absolute conclusions about specific environments or users. Note that Facebook went from serving the college population to the mainstream in just a few years, and as happened with MySpace, it may also decline in influence as new products become available. Similarly, people typically use multiple providers for distinct activities, ranging from LinkedIn for business contacts, Facebook for friends and family, ChatRoulette for meeting strangers, and pornography websites for video sex. From a personnel security standpoint, the bottom line consideration is whether any activity poses a risk to protected information such that it requires reporting and adjudication. However, future research may help guide the allocation of resources by estimating the degree of concern posed by specific activities and environments. See Part II for potential research topics.

The Second Life Experience

The authors created free Second Life personal accounts to better understand the capabilities of the virtual world and to determine if and how it might be studied. This was necessary to assess the potential for further research, and it also served to guide the formal ethnography of Second Life described in Report II. The present report describes Second Life and outlines examples of personnel security concerns, whereas Report II provides detailed findings on the activities of those who agreed to participate in the research. The images in this report were obtained using the integrated screenshot capabilities of the viewer software. All contact with other users was anonymous and occurred in public locations (i.e., akin to walking down a street and snapping pictures). The images provide a feel for what is present and how people interact, but only begin to scratch the surface of the content. Hundreds of thousands of additional images posted by Second Life users are publicly available at Flickr.com and other photography websites.

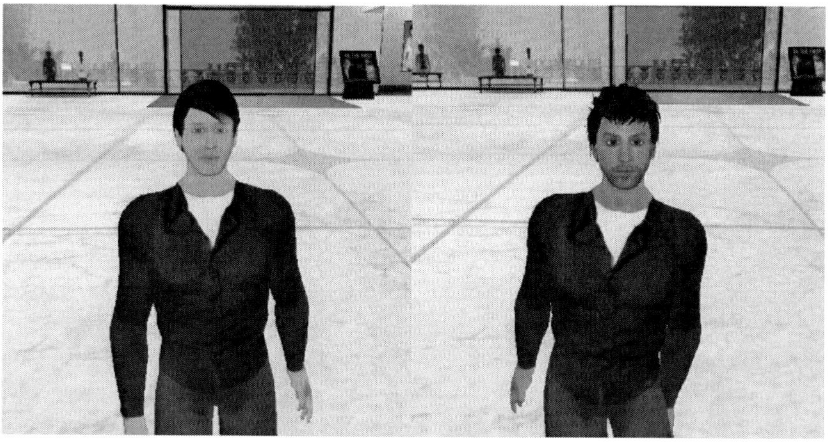

Description: A default Second Life male avatar (left), and the same avatar after upgrading the skin, hair, and eyes (right). Regular users typically upgrade and customize all aspects of their avatars' physical appearance and clothing.

Figure 1. Avatar Appearance Upgrade.

Second Life is characterized by virtual locations (at minimum a room, empty field, or open ocean) populated by characters (avatars) for the users who happen to be at the location. An avatar is an on-screen representation of each person, and may or may not physically resemble the real person (Figure 1).

Depending on the restrictions of each particular location, one's appearance can be improved, made to resemble the opposite sex, an animal, or almost anything else. Avatars are able to interact with the environment per the limitations of the software and rules of the location. At minimum one can move around, talk with others (using text and/or voice), and perform tasks related to any number of goals. Users can create as many avatars as they like. It is possible to change one's appearance in a few seconds and create multiple accounts to prevent identities from being easily connected.

Grasping the Second Life experience requires at least several visits because there is far too much to see and learn in a short period of time. Based on systematic in-world observations, the most visible users are interested in socializing, virtual fashion, music, exploration, role-play, and fantasy experimentation. These activities are supported behind the scenes by computer artists, programmers, 3D designers, and virtual shopkeepers—who may or may not participate in other activities. The in-world user-to-user economy, as used to pay for services and virtual objects, is based on Linden dollars. Linden dollars are exchangeable for real currencies across the world. The majority of users in public locations were observed at sites designed to facilitate chatting, dancing and listening to music, role-playing, shopping, and virtual sex-related activities.

Many Second Life participants appear to be attracted by the freedom of the fantasy world, and the ability to manipulate a wide range of things that generally cannot be altered in real life (e.g., gender, attractiveness, housing, weather, etc.). Some users seemingly return to the era before radio and television when entertainment relied on imagination, live performance, local pubs, and community groups. These activities are best described as a participatory alternative to reading a novel or watching a movie, with each user deciding on the story and how they want their avatar to proceed. Topics range across all those found in traditional art, fiction, and film, such as replicating popular films or TV shows, dancing (Figure 2, page 20), or interacting with original 3D art. In addition, some people indicated that they are disabled or incapacitated and use Second Life to simulate a lifestyle they cannot have in real life, plus there are special interest groups for the disabled.

While crowds of avatars can be found at many virtual clubs and hot spots, other locations are designed to replicate real-world landmarks and tourist destinations (Figure 3 and Figure 4), places of interest to a particular fan group (e.g., a space ship, a gothic vampire castle), or to create objects that would be prohibitively expensive in the real world. Linden Lab publicizes some of the best designed and unique locations in a directory, but they often have few visitors, or people visit one time and then spend hours at socially oriented places. This coincides with the comments of some users that, once they became familiar with and accustomed to Second Life, they keep returning mainly because of their friends. It is also consistent with the general interest in relationship-oriented features across other environments such as social networks and multiplayer games.

Description: Avatars looking for dance partners at Sweetheart's Ballroom Dance Club. The gray avatars are in the process of loading.

Figure 2. Avatars at a Dance Club.

Figure 3. A Second Life version of the Vietnam Veterans Memorial in Washington, D.C.

Readers should not be left with the impression that Second Life and similar products are meant only for entertainment, as graphical content can mislead some into thinking these are just games. Virtual environments have a wide range of educational, business, and professional uses. As mentioned previously, IBM has promoted their use for business meetings (Brodkin, 2008), and the vGov initiative of the National Defense University, U.S. Air Force, Homeland Security Department, and Agriculture Department seeks to develop federal virtual business environments that resemble what can now be done in Second Life (Lipowicz, 2010). Some of the most prominent productivity functions include holding classes or meetings without travel expenses, and allow physical forms of interaction for projects that benefit from visual detail. Examples of such projects include product design and engineering (e.g., collaboration between the diverse range of people working on a new aircraft, ship, or bridge), or architecture (e.g., trying several options for a new office building as seen landscaped and with surrounding buildings).

Summary

Cyber communities such as Second Life duplicate real world activities and forms of interaction in many ways. A wide range of activities are possible, and its users show enduring interest in socializing for shared experiences (e.g., exploration, music, fantasy role-play, etc.). Virtual environments also represent a step forward for business or education productivity goals requiring collaboration, as well as for efficiently completing visually-oriented tasks. In the end, social interaction always occurs between goal-driven people, regardless of the precise details and the surface appearance. It can involve computer text, voice, or video, it can occur over the telephone or face-to-face, and in Second Life, it occurs through graphical illustrations that accompany text or voice conversations.

Known Security Issues and Strategies

This report is a first step toward generating guidance for the personnel security concerns resulting from the emergence of cyberculture. While the primary longterm goal of the project is to address potential new issues and questions requiring additional research, some of the risks associated with social cyber interaction are obvious. In general, those activities that replicate real world behaviors of security concern present little apparent need for deliberation, and may only require updates to policy manuals, employee training, and the allocation of resources for enforcement. However, some differences do require a change in perspective. First, computers increase opportunities for participation in activities of potential interest (e.g., easier interaction with foreign nationals; relationships with limited information about another) so there may be more reportable events from more sources than in the past, and this could magnify the potential for exploitation. Second, the uncertainties inherent with some cyber activities present a range of probably insurmountable limitations to oversight.

False Assumptions of Anonymity and Privacy

The sometimes naïve expectation of online privacy, and the related belief that one can anonymously interact in cyberspace, underlies a wide range of risks. A given user may or may not understand how easily computer software can collect, store, and track behavior, nor understand that many parties do in fact systematically profile Internet users, but all who participate are subject to having private information obtained by others. This occurs through legal, illegal, or unethical means, and despite the intention of being cautious. For example, any online account protected only by passwords and security questions is vulnerable to hacking and social engineering, as occurred with Sarah Palin's private email account during the 2008 presidential campaign. Similarly, at one time hackers obtained databases with the account information of many Second Life users (Kirkpatrick, 2006). Another risk is that friends and associates can post incriminating information on social networks, which is more widely distributed than in the past and stored indefinitely. Finally, a business can enact changes that result in revealing more information than its users intended, as when Facebook decided to share personal data with outside businesses to enable connections between users who visit those websites (Hachman, 2010).

Merely browsing the web exposes one to a wide range of private businesses that collect and aggregate user data from public sources, such as social network accounts, blogs, email, and web browser tracking cookies. A controversy erupted in late 2010 when it was publicized that RapLeaf, Inc. had been collecting real names and detailed user characteristics, which were then transmitted to third-party advertisers. At that time, users were segmented by:

> "...household income range, age range, political leaning...gender and age of children in the household, as well as interests in topics including religion, the Bible, gambling, tobacco, adult entertainment

> and 'get rich quick' offers. In all, RapLeaf segmented people into more than 400 categories..."

In response to inquiries, RapLeaf claimed that the sharing of identifying information had been inadvertent, and also eliminated some of the more sensitive categories. Still, during the 2010 election, politicians and political organizations used RapLeaf information to send targeted ads to likely supporters (Steel, 2010). In a similar vein, privacy advocates have sought to raise awareness by compiling public location information from social networks, and then created websites such as PleaseRobMe.com and ICanStalkU.com to highlight how actual people often share information that can easily be exploited (Carton, 2010).

The cleared population faces two major risks due to assumed online anonymity and privacy, including: (1) potential exploitation through databases compiled from public or presumed secure information that track identities, jobs, activities, and associates, and (2) potentially greater willingness to share sensitive information with other people. On the first point, hostile parties can use databases to systematically seek out controlled information and target those most vulnerable to exploitation. As it is impossible to fully control the personal information that appears on the Internet, or the choices of friends, family, and associates to post information, the most practical security strategy is to develop awareness, guidance, and training programs for safe participation. In the examples below and in many other situations, the security implications can be quite different if an activity is linked to one's real identity. The second point, of how online interaction is associated with disinhibition or depersonalization, is discussed in Part II of the present report. Further research is required to assess whether cleared individuals are in fact more willing to disclose sensitive information, or more accident prone, through cyber interaction than with traditional forms of communication.

Cybersecurity, Cyber Crime, and Counterintelligence

Personnel security measures seek to protect sensitive national security information against loss, compromise, espionage, and other threats, but computer technology has widened the scope of potential risks. For example, a PERSEREC review of changes in espionage points out that the Internet has made it possible for terrorist organizations to form virtual international communities; provides easy access to large libraries of training and political documents; and allows users to employ hacking for communication and to avoid detection (Herbig, 2008). The overall impact of computers has been so significant that Steven Chabinsky, then Deputy Assistant Director of the FBI Cyber Division, called the cyber threat "one of the greatest concerns of the 21st century" (2009).

The procedures designed to combat attempts by foreign powers to obtain secure and protected information are described as counterintelligence, but the cyber threat extends well beyond spying and foreign powers. In 2010, Dennis Blair, Director of National Intelligence stated that cybersecurity and counterintelligence efforts were being integrated to improve coverage for the full range of threats. Similarly, the Naval Criminal Investigative Service (NCIS) Cyber Department integrates law enforcement and counterintelligence information (NCIS, 2010). These more generalized responses are required because hostile actions can be functionally identical regardless of an attacker's motivation. For example, one might employ hacking or social engineering to obtain access to a secure computer for personal gain (e.g., theft, blackmail, fraud, and other crimes), commercial gain (e.g., unfair business competition, illegal research and development advantages), or to undermine national security (e.g., obtaining protected information, terrorism, cyber warfare).

Responding to plainly illegal hostile cyber activities often involves a straightforward approach. Specifically, many cyber crimes committed for accessing secured computer systems are merely updates to older confidence (con) games and techniques. Gordon Snow (2010), Assistant Director of the FBI, indicated that some of the most prominent criminal activities associated with social networking websites include social engineering (misrepresentation to gain another's confidence), fraud schemes (simple lies about a product, service, investment, etc.), and phishing scams (attempts to make a user believe information is from a trusted source when it is not). When such crimes occur, the perpetrators are prosecuted through the criminal justice system using the existing standard for a given crime.

The appropriate personnel security strategy for hostile cyber threats is also often straightforward; as cyber interaction largely parallels that of the real world. For example, cyber participants should obviously report any events suggesting attempted espionage, such as abnormal romantic interest on a dating website from a foreign national when the other party might know that one has access to valuable controlled information. Similarly, the current standards used to assess personal responsibility and judgment should be applied to the nuanced negative outcomes of hostile cyber activities. To illustrate, a victim of social engineering might be considered untrustworthy after being persuaded to accept fake money orders from an international party and experiencing severe credit problems as a result.

Foreign Cyber Contacts and Associates

Cyber environments largely duplicate existing personnel security concerns for foreign contacts and associates. Prior to presenting examples of foreign contact in Second Life, the concerns presented in the Adjudicative Guidelines for Foreign Influence, Foreign Preference, and Outside Activities are shown below.

> **Guideline B - Foreign Influence:** Foreign contacts and interests may be a security concern if the individual has divided loyalties or foreign financial interests, may be manipulated or induced to help a foreign person, group, organization, or government in a way that is not in U.S. interests, or is vulnerable to pressure or coercion by any foreign interest. Adjudication under this Guideline can and should consider the identity of the foreign country in which the foreign contact or financial interest is located, including, but not limited to, such considerations as whether the foreign country is known to target United States citizens to obtain protected information and/or is associated with a risk of terrorism.
>
> **Guideline C - Foreign Preference:** When an individual acts in such a way as to indicate a preference for a foreign country over the United States, then he or she may be prone to provide information or make decisions that are harmful to the interests of the United States.
>
> **Guideline L - Outside Activities:** Involvement in certain types of outside employment or activities is of security concern if it poses a conflict of interest with an individual's security responsibilities and could create an increased risk of unauthorized disclosure of classified information.

Each of these guidelines is followed by a range of conditions that pertain to contact or association with foreign nationals.

Figure 4 (page 26) shows a group of avatars socializing in a Second Life version of Moscow's Red Square. This is only one of numerous locations in Second Life that reproduce real places across the world. As many users tend to congregate in locations thematically related to their home countries, a user targeting a specific country might log in during peak usage hours for the local time zone (daylight or after work) and visit associated locations (e.g., Red Square for Russia, the Eiffel Tower for France, etc.). Note that locations are typically developed and controlled at the discretion of private owners, so there can be more than one active version of any given real location. At the time this image was captured, several public Russian language text and voice conversations were in progress. Users must share a common language to interact with these apparent Russians or other foreign nationals with ease;

however, Second Life has an integrated text translation feature. Additionally, foreign language classes, likely with teachers of uncertain nationality, are conducted in Second Life.

Figure 4. Avatars Playing Games and Conversing in a Version of Moscow's Red Square.

Socializing with apparent foreign nationals presents obvious concerns, such as making it much easier to find and target specific countries, but other implicit assumptions do change in this environment. Specifically, (1) each user has full control over their appearance and apparent identity, and (2) barring hacking, the only way to learn another's real identity or personal facts is if the user chooses to share verifiable information, such as a name, email address, phone number, or website. The default status involves deep ambiguity about how to interpret the identity and motives of other users. As also occurs in blogs, text discussion groups, or chat rooms, some purported foreigners may pretend to be foreign to brush up on a rusty language learned in high school, imitate a character from a film, or because they want to see how average people respond to a cultural stereotype (e.g., be "a fish out of water"). Subsequently, the virtual location, a user's appearance, and the language used for communication are not proof of being foreign, and in general the true identity cannot be confirmed. Additional problems can arise among new users who rely on their real world identities, for they may not be aware of the diverse motivations of others and be subject to easy manipulation, extortion, or fraud.

Virtual Government

With the rise of the Internet, many governmental resources and functions are now available online. While any activities undertaken for internal government usage conform to existing security requirements and require access control measures, those involving the general public must occur through open websites and systems. Subsequently, government entry into cyber environments reproduces the personnel security considerations involved with conventional public interaction.

In 2007, the Maldives and Estonia opened official virtual embassies in Second Life (Maldives Mission, 2010; Riley, 2007), both intended for national promotion and to facilitate contact with other countries that do not have physical diplomatic facilities. The Estonian embassy was visited for research. It features a multistoried building with areas dedicated to travel, meetings, and cultural exhibitions. A conference area has facilities for audio-visual presentations. Figure 5 shows the travel visa application kiosk, which provides a link to a conventional website. While international universities and overseas users are extremely common in Second Life, locations intended for official government business appear to be relatively rare. Other examples of content related to diplomacy include a detailed representation of the Swedish Embassy in Washington D.C. that does not provide official services (Simmons, 2007), and a 220-member user group dedicated to assisting real governments to enter virtual worlds.

Description: The visa application kiosk at the Estonian Embassy in Second Life. The counter to the right is for the Estonian Ministry of Foreign Affairs.

Figure 5. Visa Application Kiosk.

Logically, virtual embassies and official government offices could duplicate many security concerns known to affect real embassies, such as facilitating espionage by recruiting visitors as potential intelligence agents. For example, a helpful cyber travel guide might supply a message for delivery to a real world location, turning an innocent tourist into an unwitting and thoroughly unsuspected courier. However, there is no known evidence that such activities actually take place, and the current implementations seem to more closely resemble promotional websites than real embassies. Also, ambiguity cuts both ways, whereby visitors may prove to be unreliable or not useful if real activities are perceived to be part of a game.

Conclusions: Cybersecurity Issues

The social activities made possible in cyber environments clearly reproduce existing cybersecurity concerns, and when the identity of another party is known, participation should be subject to the same reporting requirements, investigative attention, and adjudicative review as real world events. If one maintains "close and continuing" contact with a known foreign national or contacts a foreign government through a cyber environment, then it should be reported. Existing questionnaires, investigation, and adjudication documents may require updating to emphasize that cyber environments are subject to current reporting standards, but that do not exceed ordinary requirements for anonymous, isolated, routine, and uneventful physical foreign contact.

Ultimately, the majority of virtual encounters with purported foreigners are probably not worth formal personnel security consideration. This is because there is often no way to confirm the identity of contacts, let alone gain the cooperation of consciously anonymous "foreign" parties who, conversely, could also portray themselves as US citizens to avoid reporting requirements. Other than through self-reports there is no known and practical way for third parties to confirm, evaluate, or monitor cyber participation of many consciously anonymous activities. As foreign governments have little reason to target random individuals, and only minimal information can be gained without a verifiable real world identity, investigation and review of consciously anonymous interaction may often result in dead ends. Future research must assess the costs and benefits of expanded investigation requirements, but in the interim all participants in this sort of cyber environment should receive briefings on the risks and risk mitigation strategies.

Sexual Behavior and Personal Conduct

Personnel security vetting criteria have always considered character and responsibility. For example, when a clearance applicant lies to cover up a minor misdeed, such as a misdemeanor arrest or unpaid debt, it often presents a greater concern for adjudication than the original misdeed. This is because the applicant has consciously violated the terms of employment, has a continuing need to hide the original misdeed, and has created a need to hide the new lie. While many cyber activities duplicate existing personal conduct considerations about lies, character, and covering up issues, the uncertainties of cyber environments limit the conclusions that can be drawn. This is because some activities are not precisely illegal or not precisely lies, for they can be characterized as humor, entertainment, fantasies, or other activities that have no bearing on real world conduct.

The diversity of Second Life, again, provides exceptionally vivid examples of how personnel security concerns for sexual behavior and personal conduct migrate to and are affected by cyber communities. Note, however, that independent sex-oriented virtual environments such as the Utherverse Red Light Center are available, and sexually explicit role-play was once so open and aggressive on a particular World of Warcraft server that it led to a crackdown by the publisher (Parrish, 2010). For context, the concerns of the Adjudicative Guidelines (2005) for Sexual Behavior and Personal Conduct are reproduced here.

> **Guideline D - Sexual Behavior:** Sexual behavior that involves a criminal offense, indicates a personality or emotional disorder, reflects lack of judgment or discretion, or which may subject the individual to undue influence or coercion, exploitation, or duress can raise questions about an individual's reliability, trustworthiness and ability to protect classified information. No adverse inference concerning the standards in the Guideline may be raised solely on the basis of the sexual orientation of the individual.
>
> **Guideline K - Personal Conduct:** Conduct involving questionable judgment, lack of candor, dishonesty, or unwillingness to comply with rules and regulations can raise questions about an individual's reliability, trustworthiness and ability to protect classified information. Of special interest is any failure to provide truthful and candid answers during the security clearance process or any other failure to cooperate with the security clearance process.

Second Life allows for customizations that simulate physical world activities. Some of these include dancing, skiing, swimming, and riding in roller coasters or boats. To initiate these activities, the participant selects an object and then the software takes control and begins to animate the avatar, plus the user can often control movements through a menu. Simulated sex between avatars is a now common customization. Virtual sex, or cybersex, involves talking about sex either through typing or voice chat in conjunction with graphically detailed and animated depictions of sex. The simulated acts span those of pornography, extending to nonmainstream and taboo activities such as rape fantasies and bestiality. Other practices include voluntarily entering master and slave relationships, and those soliciting payment as a virtual escort or prostitute who receives Linden dollars for participation in fantasy activities. All of the above activities are legal.

Simulated pedophilia requires special attention because it has lead to widespread international concern. At one time, some adult Second Life users changed their appearance to look like children, known as "age play," and engaged in violent or sexual activities (Terdiman, 2006). This may also provide a loophole for accessing otherwise illegal child pornography, as real photographs of children can be imported into the software and then manipulated to closely resemble actual children. Simulated pedophilia was banned in the United States through the 1996 Child Pornography Prevention Act, but the law was overturned as overly broad in a 2002 Supreme Court ruling. Following this, in 2007 Germany began aggressively tracking and prosecuting simulated pedophilia in Second Life (Francescani & Kucharz, 2007). Linden Lab subsequently enhanced its enforcement of existing policies to eliminate age play, and one of the major age play content providers sought to move to an alternate virtual world (Reuters, 2008).

Personnel security standards for sexual conduct have evolved greatly over several decades, and while not entirely clear, it seems unlikely that they would be applied to simulations between consenting adults meant for private entertainment. It is obviously understood that other forms of sexual entertainment, including pornographic magazines, videos, and websites, phone sex, and interactive video sex are widely available, and in isolation they have no apparent personnel security relevance. Subsequently, the standards for online sex related activities should be similar to established practices. Examples that parallel known concerns include:

1) Any sexual content or activity can generate some risk of extortion when the real identities of those involved are known. For example, a 27-year-old man was convicted of trying to blackmail a 14-year-old girl into providing pornographic videos after he obtained explicit

photos, and another man in search of explicit photos broke into 3,200 email accounts by resetting user passwords by using information shared on Facebook (McMillan, 2011).

2) Ongoing interaction with identifiable people, or when interaction has lead to physical contact, appear to be subject to existing reporting requirements for romantic relationships.
3) If virtual and physical prostitution occurs with the same individual, virtual sex activities might be of interest during an investigation to determine the extent of the relationship.
4) Simulated pedophilia and simulated child abuse are illegal in some countries, and US law may not yet be settled, so participation presents an apparent risk of international prosecution and blackmail.

Summary

This section presented examples of how current personnel security issues and coverage requirements can directly transfer to cyber activities, and where ambiguities can limit the potential for investigation or adjudicative review. Cyber environments clearly duplicate many real world security concerns, and subsequently should receive systematic and serious consideration. However, these activities should not receive greater attention than real world activities, nor is it worthwhile investigating those lacking relevance or likely to result in dead ends.

Experience has shown that it can be difficult to formulate effective cyber polices, even when it is known that a given activity poses at least some risk. For example, the US Marine Corps briefly banned access to social networks, describing them as "...a proven haven for malicious actors and content and are particularly high risk due to information exposure, user generated content, and targeting by adversaries...," (Marines, 2009), but the ban was lifted a few months later and a new memo instead outlined guidance for responsible, appropriate, and legal use of Internet resources (Marines, 2010). The immediately actionable principles and recommendations derived from Part I of the report are presented below.

1) Action should be taken to increase awareness across the personnel security community that cyber activities can be functionally identical to real world activities and can present similar risks. Cyber activities that are reportable per the current Adjudicative Guidelines should be explicitly considered along with real world activities. The examples suggest several requirements and strategies for further consideration:

a) Cyber relationships with foreign nationals or virtual romantic partners, when the real world identity of a cleared individual is shared, might be investigated and adjudicated per the existing standards for these topics.
b) Any experience of hostile cyber threats (i.e., from foreign parties, extortionists, or others who know a user's real world identity) should be reported and investigated on an equal footing with real world reporting of such activities.
c) Participation in simulated child pornography or simulated child abuse may be reportable because of international laws and the associated potential for blackmail.
d) It is unlikely that reviewing intentionally anonymous contact with purported foreigners, fantasy romantic partners, or others will be possible, productive, or cost effective. This is because people can continuously create multiple new anonymous identities, there is no known way to determine the identities of other anonymous parties without affecting general privacy rights, and most actions have no apparent personnel security relevance.

2) All established cybersecurity topics, such as cyber money laundering, hacking, gang activity, and organized crime, should be systematically reviewed to update personnel security reporting and evaluation guidance.
3) No policy, reporting, or enforcement changes should be made to address novel cyber activities that do not derive directly from existing real-world personnel security standards, unless the changes are supported by empirical evidence.
4) As outlined in Part II of the present report, personnel security policymakers should address how best to evaluate and manage participation in cyber environments. The core needs are to:
    a) Define new and unique cyber topics of potential personnel security interest. Part II presents a range of topics for consideration, and is meant to guide research for this need.
    b) Determine the costs and benefits associated with covering new topics.
        I. Assess potential for collecting and validating data, considering anonymous participation, the dark web (private, unsearchable content), hijacked content (content copied, stolen, or taken out of context), content stored internationally,

and respect for the privacy and civil rights of the general population.

II. Generate self reporting requirements and clearly specify investigative boundaries.

Part I provided an overview of cyberculture in the general cybersecurity context, outlined important considerations and unanswered questions for personnel security, provided detailed examples of how cyber activities can duplicate known real world issues, and listed immediately actionable recommendations. Part II sketches the state of research knowledge to look to the future and how move forward in responding to the threats posed by cyberculture with greater precision and more comprehensively.

PART II: SCIENTIFIC CONTEXT AND RESEARCH GUIDANCE

Cyberculture and Psychology

This section presents examples of the logic and research evidence for how cyber activities might result in personnel security, psychological, and workplace concerns—and therefore helps guide future research. Society is in the process of learning how rapidly evolving technologies such as personal computers, cell phones, mobile electronics, and wireless network access affect culture, how they solve old problems, and how they create new concerns. Research to understand the impact of these technologies can only occur as products become available and popular. There are no known data on the psychological impact of cyberculture among potential security clearance applicants or current holders, so targeted research is required. The most prominent concerns for personnel security appear to fall into two broad categories: (1) how the ability to manipulate personal information and control virtual relationships may affect standards for real-life loyalty, reliability, and trustworthiness, and (2) how constant availability may enable or promote impulse control disorders and addiction. The examples below highlight the need for focused research on cyberculture, psychology, and personnel security, but should not be regarded as an exhaustive list of all topics of potential concern[2].

Computer Mediated Relationships and Disinhibition

A common observation is that people interact differently in cyberspace than offline, such as being more willing to disclose private information about the self, express secret emotions, engage in virtual sexual intimacy, express harsh criticism of strangers, willfully disrupt discussions, etc. For example, research has shown that frequent online chatters are more likely to disclose intimate and personal details than nonfrequent chatters (Leung, 2002). McKenna and Bargh (2000) describe this effect as deindividuation, and Riva (2002) cites work indicating that the absence of face-to-face cues leads to argumentative and destructive interactions, while Suler (2004) calls this phenomenon the *online disinhibition effect.* Furthermore, Suler's detailed analysis separates *benign* disinhibition, including reduced fear, shyness, and greater generosity, from *toxic* activities such as rudeness, anger, hatred, and accessing violent or pornographic material.

Disinhibition is a useful concept for summarizing how interpersonal interaction often changes in cyberspace. Making social contact and forming or maintaining relationships from behind a computer display facilitates things that are not possible or practical in the real world. There is no eye contact, body language, or other behavioral evidence of a person's mood and attitude. It becomes easy to present oneself as an expert, impersonate a public figure, and lie about location, job, gender, or age. People can express taboo or bigoted thoughts, and say things that would offend friends and family. Furthermore, a person need not respond to others immediately, and so can more precisely calculate and construct answers. McKenna and Bargh (2000) reviewed research comparing virtual versus face-to-face interaction and summarized differences that remain central today. They concluded that computers permit: (1) being anonymous, (2) developing relationships regardless of physical distance, (3) forming relationships without consideration of physical appearance, and (4) interacting without regard for an immediate response, such as through email and text messaging. Several examples of how these changes interact with potential security risks are presented below.

Openness and Risk Taking

McKenna and Bargh (2000) discuss how the Internet creates a safe zone and blank slate for fantasy experimentation. One can create many alternate versions of the self, with the possibility of exploring fringe politics, homosexuality, and other activities that may lead to stigmatization among certain cultural groups. Their prior empirical studies found that, when online, people tend to present idealized selves and favor strangers better than when meeting the same person face to face. However, they also note that a fantasy self might potentially lead to delusional or unrealistic real-world behavior; and as anonymous conversations lack the consequences of real life activities, they often create a false sense of interaction (Shapira, et al., 2003). From a personnel security standpoint, if a great deal or the majority of communication is unconstrained by the repercussions of personal disclosure, there is a possibility that this may lead to forming relationships abnormally fast and expressing thoughts without restraint. In turn, this could ultimately lead to the unintentional disclosure of sensitive or classified information.

From an ordinary cultural and psychological standpoint, meeting new people, exploring unfamiliar cultures, and trying new experiences are generally perceived as having positive consequences. In contrast, personnel security background screening criteria require the reporting of, and therefore potentially discourage, foreign contact and association. For example, Suler's (2004) analysis of online disinhibition describes the increased willingness to disclose personal information as a "benign" effect, yet accidental disclosure (e.g., during absentminded conversations) is a significant concern with sensitive or classified information. This is compounded by the fact that cyber communities allow people to easily form relationships across national borders, with no vetting of the foreign nationals or even the possibility of determining their true identities. Similarly, if individuals engage in fantasy taboo activities and fear being discovered, they might go to great lengths to hide their interests and associations from a spouse, coworker, or employer. A Time Magazine story described how a real-life marriage that began with a meeting in an online chat room later ended amid accusations of Second Life affairs, the hiring of virtual private investigators, attempts at virtual seduction, and claims of cyber addiction (Adams, 2008). As discussed above, the potential for blackmail in cyberculture is similar to that in the conventional world, and should be consistently considered during background investigations.

Targeted personnel security research must assess how so-called "benign" disinhibition bears on unintentional disclosure of sensitive or classified information, Foreign Influence and Preference concerns, and other disqualifying behaviors from the Adjudicative Guidelines. The systematic observations of Second Life provided widespread evidence of disinhibition. Consistent with the notion of unrealistic interaction, most Second Life avatars have idealized bodies (e.g., extremely tall, fashionable, long legs, complex hairstyles) and are often hyper-masculine or hyper-feminine. "Friendships" are formed quickly and easily, but often end without notice when the one party simply deletes the other party's contact information. With regard to blackmail, some avatars informed the research staff that they were "deep undercover" when asked if friends and family knew about their involvement, introducing the risk of blackmail or exploitation. The Second Life ethnography described in Report II addresses these concerns and findings in detail.

Misrepresentation and Deception

The honesty of clearance holders is a core consideration for personnel security, as accurate information is essential for conducting a background investigation and the basis for trusting an individual with sensitive information. In contrast to how society functioned decades ago, the relative anonymity and confidentiality available online offers great opportunities for exaggeration or outright deception with regard to one's true identity and competence (Suler, 2004). People are also widely aware that cyber environments increase the potential for misleading others and believe that online deception is extremely common (Caspi & Gorsky, 2006). However, while opportunities for deception are clearly present online, the reviewed research indicates that in practice: (1) deception is not necessarily more common online than offline, (2) people tend to present themselves in an idealized but largely realistic light, but (3) deception occurs most often in anonymous communities and where there is limited potential for verifying facts or affecting everyday life (Zhao, Grasmuck, & Martin, 2008; Caspi & Gorsky, 2006). From a personnel security standpoint, it is important to understand why and when deception does occur, and how misrepresentation varies by context. The reasons are presented below.

Cyber communities that focus on the real world are rooted in conventional standards for disclosure and honesty. When a person seeks a continuing and real relationship, deception is counterproductive because it will undermine trust if discovered. The core goals of dating websites and social networks are largely incompatible with outright lies, so the distortion in these communities tends to be used to put oneself in the best light, such as being friendly, popular, successful, well-rounded, and having good taste (Zhao, et al., 2008). This is consistent with research indicating that increased use of Facebook is correlated with narcissism and low self-esteem (Mehdizadeh, 2010). However, social networks facilitate another sort of misrepresentation through the reportedly common practice of creating multiple personas and false identities (Riva, 2002; Subrahmanyam & Greenfield, 2008; Boutin, 2010). These can be used to separate information available to particular circles of associates (e.g., friends vs. family vs. workplace) and shape the impression given to contacts. It is not clear whether this practice constitutes a form of misrepresentation important for personnel security vetting, but there may be a legitimate need to know if employees are leading double lives.

Cyber communities with optional anonymity (e.g., Second Life, games, and blogs) allow the greatest potential for misrepresentation. For example, claims of having homosexual or nonmainstream sexual preferences have been found to be less common on Facebook than in chat rooms and anonymous environments (Zhao, et al., 2008). There is often no practical way to determine whether such individuals are truly interested in participation, or if they have an ulterior motive such as trying to stimulate discussion or generate a reaction. Conventional ethical standards appear to change the most when there is anonymity and few consequences for deception, such as with some multiplayer games. In the online word game Lexulous (similar to Scrabble) users frequently misrepresent their competence by using external scrabble solver engines that unscramble letters and display possible words during competitive games. Although this practice would be considered cheating in a real-world tournament, it is not considered unethical by the users in this context (Slatalla, 2009).

Returning to the project goal of understanding how cyberculture may affect personnel security interests in character, reliability, and judgment, questions requiring future research include: (1) whether general cultural standards for honesty might be affected by extensive, long-term interaction among those who do not value honesty, such that dishonesty adversely affects the workplace, and (2) whether some individuals might become confused about what constitutes appropriate workplace vs. cyber behavior. The reviewed publications suggest that most people tend to adopt similar standards and approaches both online and offline (Caspi & Gorsky, 2006; Subrahmanyam & Greenfield, 2008; Zhao, et al., 2008), but there are hints that cyber participation may be associated with measurable changes in ethics or morality. For example, a survey found that frequent participants in discussion groups lied more often than infrequent participants; and in contrast with real life lies, online lies were primarily seen as enjoyable and not associated with negative emotions (Caspi & Gorsky, 2006). It is also not clear whether and how particularly malicious individuals might use cyber environments for gain over those users who maintain their real world personas.

Hostility and Aggression

Participants in cyber communities have long known that some people become much more hostile, aggressive, and blunt online than they would be in real life. In discussion groups, unchecked criticism or anger is known as "flaming," and mentioning controversial topics to stir up a response is known as "trolling." These are examples of toxic online disinhibition per Suler's (2004) analysis, and they occur in a wide range of communities, including user comments about news stories, political discussions, special-interest blogs, social networks, games, and chat rooms. The associated personnel security concerns are that cyberculture might lead to an increase in real-world aggression, or that cultural acceptance of overt hostility could affect workplace management.

Cyberbullying involves using electronic devices for intentional and repeated aggression against those who cannot mount an effective defense (Smith, Mahdavi, Carvalho, & Tippett, 2006). It has received extensive legal and media attention in conjunction with suicides. For example, Lori Drew, the mother of a former friend of 13-year-old Megan Meier, created a false social network profile and befriended the girl, but then later turned on her in revenge for perceived mistreatment of her child, which drove Megan to take her own life (Collins, 2008). Following Megan's suicide, Lori Drew was tried and convicted of three misdemeanors, but the case was eventually dismissed by the judge (Zavis, 2009). Similarly, five Massachusetts students were criminally charged for systematic bullying (both cyber and conventional) associated with the suicide of Phoebe Prince, a 15-year-old ninth-grader from Ireland (Bazelon, 2010). Surveys of urban Canadian adolescents by Li (2006, 2007) indicate that about a quarter of junior high students have been victims of cyberbullying, and almost 15% have themselves been cyberbullies (12% of females, 22% of males).

While the motives for bullying are similar in any situation, computer technology makes it easier to attack anonymously, take embarrassing pictures, create critical websites, store information that cannot be removed, and widely distribute hostile messages. The next generation of security clearance holders will have lived through such experiences, and events that might have once been "skeletons in the closet" could become widely known and permanently available. Li (2007) notes that many adolescents are naïve about appropriate safety strategies for cyberspace, and often do not report bullying to adults. Subsequently, background investigations may soon uncover new types and a greater volume of potentially derogatory information, and being a bully or being bullied may have longer lasting effects. Research is necessary to determine the implications and formulate an appropriate response.

Another concern involves participation in violent video games, which have been widely researched for potentially increasing real-world aggression and negatively impacting school performance (Gentile, Lynch, Linder, &

Walsh, 2004; Ivory & Kalyanaraman, 2007; Konijn, Bijvank, & Bushman, 2007). For example, Konijn et al. had adolescent boys with low educational ability play violent or nonviolent video games and then later asked them to "play sounds for a partner" when they were told that the volume could be loud enough to permanently damage the partner's hearing. Those who played violent games and wishfully identified with aggressive, remorseless game characters were more likely to play damaging sounds even when not provoked. This seems to be of particular interest to the military, where unjustified violence against civilians during combat can lead to increased resistance and undermine the chances for a successful campaign. For example, in late 2003 U.S. military personnel abused and tortured prisoners at Abu Ghraib in Iraq, and also took graphic photographs of their actions (Hersh, 2004). As a potentially contributing factor, the role of violent video games should be evaluated.

Impulse Control and Cyber Addiction

Cyberculture facilitates a wide range of activities and forms of social interaction that can be difficult to find or organize in the real world. These are often done in private and without feedback from friends or family, and relationships can exist purely through computers. If desired, a person can use computers for remote employment, shopping, socializing, and entertainment. A concern in the scientific and popular press is that computer-related technologies can lead to cyber addiction. Cyber addiction is a behavioral addiction that entails excessive use of specific cyber environments or cyber space in general, resulting in negative psychosocial and professional impairments to a person's life, to include personal, school, and work difficulties (Caplan, 2002; Caplan, Williams, & Yee, 2009; Beard & Wolf, 2001; Shapira, Goldsmith, Keck, Khosla, & McElroy, 2000). The notion of cyber addiction is relatively new, but it has received a great deal of attention in the scientific literature. Other terms for this phenomenon include compulsive computer use or pathological Internet use, and share common features with impulse control, substance abuse, and obsessive-compulsive disorders from DSM-IV. An influential editorial written by Jerald Block in the *American Journal of Psychiatry* in 2008, made a case for why cyber addiction should be included in the *Diagnostic and Statistical Manual of Mental Disorders,* 5th Ed. He argued that because the symptoms involve excessive use, withdrawal, tolerance, and negative repercussions, it should be added to the spectrum of recognized impulse control disorders.

Poor impulse control, or taking action without consideration of the longer-term consequences, appears to be associated with a wide range of potentially disqualifying behaviors in the Adjudicative Guidelines, including psychological conditions, criminal activity, financial mismanagement, drunk driving, and more. In all manifestations, with or without addiction per se, this deficit can undermine individuals' reliability, judgment, and trustworthiness to handle and safeguard classified information. Importantly, however, certain individuals may exhibit problems in some contexts (such as online games) but not others (such as finances), so a broader range of activities may require consideration during investigations and adjudication. For example, a Subject might honestly not report any psychological, criminal, or financial problems per the current Standard Form 86 (SF-86) questions during a background investigation, but still play games during work breaks, evenings, and weekends for upwards of 30-40 hours per week. This could impact alertness on the job and create direct risks when operating complex equipment, driving vehicles, or using weapons. In 2008 a commuter train engineer sent a text message 22 seconds before a crash that killed 24 people and caused $10.6 million in damages. He had previously been caught twice on the job with a cell phone (CNN, 2009).

A large-scale epidemiological study of problematic cyber use (Aboujaoude, Koran, Gamel, Large, & Serpe, 2006) found that between 3.7% to 13.7% of U.S. adult Internet users met one or more diagnostic criteria for impulse control disorders, such as feeling that personal relationships have suffered as a result of excessive cyber use, feeling preoccupied by the Internet when offline, finding it difficult to stay away from the Internet for several days at a time, etc. Some have outlined theoretical frameworks and implications for cyber addiction. Block (2008) characterizes cyber addiction as involving online and/or offline computer usage, and consisting of at least three subtypes: excessive gaming, preoccupations with online sexual behavior, and email/text messaging. The three subtypes of cyber addiction all share the following characteristics common to addictive disorders: (1) excessive use, associated with a loss of sense of time or a neglect of basic biological drives, (2) withdrawal, accompanied by feelings of anger, tension, and depression when the computer is inaccessible, (3) tolerance, including the need for better computer equipment, more software, and more hours of use, and (4) negative repercussions, including disagreements, lying, poor achievement, social isolation, and fatigue.

Online multiplayer games clearly illustrate the potential impact of heavy or addictive computer use. Hardcore gamers have been known to play all night long, skip meals, fail to exercise, and have even died during extended play sessions (Anderson, 2001; Nalwa & Anand, 2003; Young, 1998; BBC News, 2005). Users of massively multiplayer online role-playing games (MMORPGs) such as World of Warcraft and Everquest often play in a fashion that many consider to be excessive. Research indicates that the design of World of Warcraft is consistent with behavioral conditioning principles for encouraging more play and longer play—as one goal of the developer is to prolong player subscriptions and increase profits (Ducheneaut, et al., 2006). A survey of 7,000 EverQuest 2 players found that an average player is 31.16 years old and plays an average of 26.86 hours a week (Williams, Yee, & Caplan, 2008). Ng and Wiemer-Hastings (2005) reported that 34% of surveyed MMORPG users played for 21-40 hours per week and 11% played for more than 40 hours per week, but only 4% and 2% of non-MMORPG players fell into the same hourly categories. Finally, Yee (2004) reports that 50% of MMORPG players consider themselves addicted.

Summary

This section presented examples of why personnel security needs to consider the impact of cyberculture on employees' fitness to handle classified information and occupy sensitive positions. However, these examples must not be viewed as the final word or specific recommendations, because necessary data are not yet available. A long history of research in personality and social psychology indicates that the impact of any medium varies between individuals and situations, and is shaped by goals and motivations (McKenna & Bargh, 2000). Subsequently, as with all other behaviors, cyber participation must be examined using the whole person concept and with appropriate consideration of mitigating factors.

Empirical research must assess if and how cyber involvement can result in demonstrable negative real world consequences. For example, reliance on anonymous relationships or adopting potentially reckless and unethical norms may result in inappropriate workplace behavior. Having a pattern of weak one-sided relationships may lead to unrealistic expectations for control and a desire to avoid unpleasant situations or responsibility. The adoption of cyber world norms may translate into workplace behaviors of security concern, such as being secretive, breaking rules, and lying. Finally, cyber addiction poses a likely security risk because of close parallels to impulse control disorders known to affect judgment, reliability, and trustworthiness, such as gambling and alcoholism.

Cyberculture and Maladaptive Spillover

A core goal of this project is to determine if and how maladaptive involvement in cyberculture might have significant negative consequences for the personal and professional lives of clearance holders that could impact personnel security. While the section above described how cyberculture can affect cognitive outcomes, this section reviews findings on the relationship between cyber use and mental and physical health outcomes, as well as employee behavior in the workplace. Good mental and physical health is important because both are conditions of employment for many sensitive positions (e.g., Department of Defense Personnel Reliability Program [PRP] positions requiring employees to work with nuclear weapons; Department of Defense, 2006). Workplace behavior must be considered to assess whether cyber behavior might negatively affect judgment, as poor judgment in the workplace can be a serious security risk requiring prompt attention. It is presently unclear whether cyber involvement occurring outside work significantly affects workplace behavior, so this question requires exploration.

Mental Health Outcomes

Scientific research examining the impact of cyber involvement on mental health outcomes can be divided into two categories. Type I studies characterize cyber use by the average number of hours per week spent in cyberspace. These studies select participants through questionnaires on their cyber involvement and various indications of mental health functioning (e.g., mood, self-esteem, etc.). During the data analytic phase, the time spent in cyber space is correlated with evaluations of mental health functioning, and/or statistical modeling techniques are used to understand whether the time spent in cyber space and demographic characteristics predict mental health functioning. Type II studies define cyber use as the presence of clinical symptoms descriptive of compulsive-impulsive spectrum disorders from the DSM-IV. These studies typically examine individuals with diagnosed cyber addiction problems, detected either upon seeking counseling or through those who happen to have extreme scores on measures of cyber addiction. Participants in Type II studies fill out questionnaires about their cyber involvement or participate in detailed interviews on the experience of cyber addiction. Results from Type II studies can only be generalized to individuals suffering from diagnosed cyber addiction.

The findings of Type I studies are most relevant for estimating and understanding spillover in the population of clearance holders, whereas the findings from Type II studies will have limited applicability for most functional employees. This is because only a fraction of individuals experience clinical symptoms of cyber addiction (Aboujaoude et al., 2006). However, the clinical cases presented in Type II studies are helpful for illustrating cyber addiction in detail and the potential risks facing the cleared workforce.

The consensus findings of Type I studies are that the amount of time spent in cyberspace is correlated with diminished impulse control, depressed mood, loneliness, reduced social support, low self-esteem, and withdrawal from family activities (e.g., Armstrong, Phillips, & Saling, 2000; Caplan, 2002; Davis, Flett, & Besser, 2002; Kraut et al., 1998; Meerkerk, 2007). In other words, the more time individuals spend in cyberspace, the more likely they are to report experiencing these negative mental health outcomes. Nearly all of these Type I studies did not differentiate between specific and generalized cyber use (Davis, 2001). "Specific" cyber use refers to the amount of time spent using a given cyber environment (e.g., Facebook, World of Warcraft, or Second Life), whereas generalized use refers to the overall amount of time spent in cyberspace. It is likely that some of the negative mental health effects observed in Type I studies pertain to particular types of cyber environments (e.g., the massively multiplayer online role-playing game EverQuest 2; Ng & Wiemer-Hastings, 2005). Future research should systematically distinguish between specific and generalized cyber use.

The findings of Type II studies suggest that, compared to normal people, cyber addicts are more likely to experience mood and anxiety disorders such as depression and bipolar disorder, substance use disorders, personality disorders, emotional distress, loneliness, family problems, and withdrawal symptoms when their cyber access is taken away (Black, Belsare, & Schlosser, 1999; Chappell, Eatough, Davies, & Griffiths, 2006; Morahan-Martin & Schumacker, 2000; Shapira et al., 2000; Young & Rogers, 1998). To illustrate, Shapira et al. (2000) interviewed people who experienced problematic cyber use and spent more than 30 hours a week in cyberspace for the past 3 years. In addition to suffering from a number of psychosocial impairments, all of the participants met the diagnostic criteria of an impulse control disorder not otherwise specified, and nearly all met the criteria for manic depression or a psychotic disorder with similar features while the others had a history of anxiety disorders, substance abuse problems, impulse control disorders and eating disorders.

In aggregation, the findings of Type II studies suggest that cyber addicts suffer from a great deal of psychological distress, which may not only affect their day-to-day well-being, but also their judgment in the workplace.

Converging evidence for the diminished ability to make decisions comes from a study by Immordino-Yang, McColl, Damasio, & Damasio (2009). These scientists showed that rapid exchanges of information from text messaging and microblogging (e.g., Twitter, Tumblr) websites could actually harm individuals' moral and emotional development, by not allowing users to sufficiently process information before responding. Ironically, individuals may be turning to various cyber environments to reduce psychological distress, but in doing so they withdraw from real-life social contact and only exacerbate it further (Davis, Flett, & Besser, 2002; Kim, LaRose, & Peng, 2009).

Physical Health Outcomes

Little empirical research on the associations between cyber use and physical health has been conducted; however, theoretical work published in the *Biologist* shows that excessive cyber use can harm health by reducing the amount of face-to-face contact among individuals (Sigman, 2009). Additionally, several studies have examined the relationship between cyber use and sleep (Anderson, 2001; Nalwa & Anand, 2003; Young, 1998). Finally, various media accounts suggest that in extreme cases, excessive cyber use can result in death.

In his *Biologist* article, Sigman (2009) discussed the biological implications for public health of social networking and communicating through computer-based technologies. He argued that increased reliance on computer-based communication should be considered a growing public health issue, with negative implications for eye and ear contact, gene expression, sleep efficiency, immunological changes, morbidity, and mortality. Sigman's overarching hypothesis is that by communicating with others virtually we become socially isolated from our physical networks of friends and family, which in turn makes us more vulnerable to various adverse health outcomes. Although the direct relationship between cyber communication and physical health has not been investigated longitudinally, there are well-established links between cyber use and loneliness (e.g., Kraut et al., 1998, Leung, 2002) and between loneliness and markers of health and well-being (e.g., Cohen, Doyle, Skoner, Rabin, & Gwaltney, 1997; Hawkley, Thisted, & Cacioppo, 2009; Lund, Christensen, Holstein, Due, & Osler, 2006), thereby lending credibility to Sigman's hypothesis that cyber use could harm health.

Excessive cyber use has been found to lead to the loss of sleep. In several studies comparing cyber addicts with normal controls (Anderson, 2001; Nalwa & Anand, 2003; Young, 1998), cyber addicts reported frequently losing sleep due to late night log-ins. Addicted participants would stay online until early morning hours, despite knowing they had to be at work or school early the following morning, or knowing they would feel fatigued the next day. In extreme cases, participants even reported using caffeine pills to continue their cyber use. A large number of individuals also indicated that they stopped exercising or attending to personal hygiene, and often skipped meals because of cyber use. For the present project, the research staff read several hundred stories of addiction posted by users and their family members on the On-line Gamers Anonymous (OLGA) website (www.olganon.org). The postings resonated with the published findings, through comments about suffering from a loss of sleep, lack of proper nutrition, and lack of exercise.

Finally, a number of media accounts suggest that, in extreme cases, cyber overuse can have fatal consequences. In 2008, a 15-year-old boy in Sweden collapsed and went into epileptic convulsions after playing World of Warcraft for more than 24 hours straight. Medical authorities ruled that the epileptic seizure was caused by sleep deprivation and lack of food, as well as staring at a screen and concentrating for hours on end (Fox News, 2008). A 28-year old man in South Korea died after reportedly playing an online computer game for 50 hours (BBC News, 2005), and the police reported the cause of death was heart failure stemming from exhaustion. The young man had also not been sleeping properly or eating well for a long period of time, and had been recently fired because of constantly missing work to play the game. A similar fatal case in China involved a 27-year-old man who died at an Internet café after playing a game for 32 hours (VNUnet News, 2002). Suicides have also resulted, as with a 13-year-old boy who died while trying to recreate a scene from the World of Warcraft (Fox News, 2006). His suicide note stated that he jumped from a tall building to reunite with the heroes of the game he worshipped. Another suicide occurred in Wisconsin, where a 21-year-old EverQuest addict fatally shot himself in front of his computer after being rejected by another player (Fox News, 2007). Finally, there have been several cases involving small children dying from neglect because their parents were addicted to playing online games (MSNBC News, 2007).

Workplace Outcomes

There are several ways that cyber involvement might spill over to the workplace and create personnel security risks. First and foremost, relaxed attitudes and habits for lying and rule breaking that are generally accepted in cyberspace could become more problematic in professional contexts. Second, individuals may work less than scheduled or required because of compulsions to access blocked cyber environments, or attempt to access blocked environments at work by bypassing information security barriers (Greenfield & Davis, 2002; Shapira et al., 2000; Young, 1998). This concern applies primarily to organizations that both block employee access to the relevant websites and do not permit external wireless devices at work. In contrast, those organizations that permit electronic devices face the problem of employees accessing websites through personal devices without leaving any traceable evidence. This activity subjects employees both to the potential psychological spillover resulting from addiction and the risk of inadvertent disclosure of sensitive work information.

A large number of studies have shown that cyber addiction is linked to several negative outcomes occurring both at home and in the workplace (Greenfield & Davis, 2002; Kraut et al., 1998; Morahan-Martin & Schumacher, 2000; Padilla-Walker, Nelson, Carroll, & Jensen, 2009; Young & Rogers, 1998). A national household telephone survey conducted by Aboujaoude et al. (2006) concluded that cyber use has become a consuming societal problem. Moreover, cyber addiction may be a risk factor for other behavioral and substance-related addictions that impact the workplace, such as pathological gambling and alcoholism (Black et al., 1999).

Finally, cyberspace is characterized by easy access, affordability and anonymity (King, 1999), and is, therefore, effective for concealing pornographic activities from coworkers (Cavaglion, 2008; Young, 2008). Online sexual preoccupation can affect the workplace when employees access pornography at work. It was revealed that more than 30 DoD employees with high-level security clearances, employed at organizations including the National Security Agency (NSA), National Reconnaissance Office (NRO), and Defense Advanced Projects Research Agency (DARPA), have been investigated since 2002 for the possession of child pornography. Some accessed this material from government computers, and one individual had stored 93 documents, 8,400 pictures, and 200 movies (Bender, 2010). Online sexual preoccupation is risky from a personnel security standpoint for several reasons. First, it entails significant financial consequences for employers due to the loss of labor and productivity. Second, it may result in blackmail of the employee. Third, the apparent lack of impulse control on the part of an employee signals impaired judgment and poor decisionmaking ability, which could translate into difficulties in following rules or adequately protecting classified information. Finally, online communication about sex at work introduces the risks of inadvertently revealing sensitive information or being pressured to reveal sensitive information during these interactions.

Summary

This section has reviewed a wide range of evidence and research findings for how cyber participation may be associated with serious negative mental health, physical health, and workplace outcomes. Spillover effects related to reliability, trustworthiness, and judgment can be of great concern for many sensitive personnel security positions. For mental health, research suggests excessive cyber use may be associated with impulse control problems and depression, but more specific research is required. For physical health, excessive cyber use has been associated with loss of sleep, lack of exercise, poor nutrition, and even death. For the workplace, excessive use could lead to increased acceptance of rule breaking, with potential consequences for the security measures designed to protect controlled information, the loss of productivity, and potential exposure to legal liabilities. Future research needs to address the overall impact of spillover and provide actionable recommendations.

General Discussion

This report has outlined the changes facing society with the emergence of cybercultures; described the purposes and capabilities of several cyber environments; presented detailed examples from the virtual social environment, Second Life; highlighted why cyber behaviors can be of personnel security concern; and reviewed scientific literature on the psychological and potentially adverse real world impact of participation. Cyber environments are playing an ever larger role in modern life, seemingly because they provide so many benefits for socialization, business, shopping, entertainment, and education. However, they also expand the range of potential personnel security risks. Some risks, such as facilitating contact with foreign nationals, largely duplicate established issues and are presently reportable. Other topics requiring research include impulse control problems or addiction, physical and heath problems, and potential changes in socialization that are inconsistent with present standards for telling the truth and privacy. Data pertaining to many central personnel security questions are not yet available, so research must be conducted to generate actionable guidance.

Next Steps for the Cyberculture Research Program

Empirical research is necessary to better understand the psychological, workplace, and real life impact of cyberculture participation, as affecting personnel security. This research is in its early stages and faces several major questions. First, there are no known data on how frequently clearance holders participate in cyber communities and what behaviors they choose. Second, there are few data showing whether participation has any measurable impact on outcomes of concern to personnel security, such as judgment, reliability, and trustworthiness. Third, it is possible that any effects will change, moderate, or broaden over time as cyber communities grow and the participants settle into long-term usage patterns.

Given the above considerations, this project was planned as a multi-phase investigation to evaluate the personnel security impact and identify best practices for handling new issues that are presently unaddressed by the vetting process. The first empirical step, as presented independently in Report II, was to gather basic information on activities that are potentially relevant to the concerns specified in the Adjudicative Guidelines, and to collect feedback from cyber environment users about how participation affects their personal lives and work performance. Following this, it is necessary to learn how frequently people engage in activities of potential concern, understand if there are differences among users of different cyber environments (e.g., social networks vs. online games vs. explicitly anonymous environments, mobile activities, etc.), determine what those differences are, and generate recommendations for personnel security management.

Report II: Ethnographic Analysis of Second Life

As research progressed for Report I, it was determined that empirical research would be necessary to answer many important questions, and that the research would have different requirements than the present report. Report II uses an ethnographic approach to better understand Second Life, as available evidence indicated that its users might exhibit behaviors of personnel security concern. Ethnographic data collection methods capture the complexity of human experience. This entails watching people on their own territory, becoming immersed in their culture, building rapport to overcome disclosure barriers, and gathering information through observation, focus groups, and interviews (O'Reilly, 2004).

The Second Life ethnography was designed in coordination with a subcontractor who specializes in ethnographic methods and who has an established research presence in Second Life. Participants with characteristics similar to clearance holders (e.g., U.S. citizens, 18 or older, employed full-time, working in a professional environment, willing to accept an employment background check, etc.) were recruited, and then several methods were used to understand their Second Life activities and the impact on their real lives. Cyber activities were considered in context of the Adjudicative Guidelines, and real life spillover as related to health, relationships, functioning, and behavior in the workplace. Finally, the data were used to guide future research.

Prevalence of Risky Behaviors and Additional Recommendations

Research in progress seeks to determine the prevalence rates of behaviors of potential concern and generate best practice recommendations for investigators, adjudicators, personnel security managers, and policymakers. Some topics to be addressed include: (1) establishing the major points of awareness about the impact of cyber participation, (2) determining potential differences between types of environments, (3) proposing specific modifications to the Personnel Security Questionnaire (SF-86), (4) proposing specific changes to investigative methods and coverage, and (5) outlining considerations affecting the Adjudicative Guidelines.

Mobile and Pervasive Computing

Mobile and pervasive computing differs in important ways from traditional systems, and therefore requires special consideration. First, people are now vulnerable to exploitation by hostile parties while moving about, either because of their own actions or the capabilities of others. Second, some may grow so dependent on computers that heavy usage (e.g., many hours per day) becomes common. Finally, people who share constantly may find traditional interpersonal interaction to be difficult. In this vein, police have reported that domestic disturbance calls resulting from hostile or abusive text messages—with no physical contact—were once nonexistent but are now common. Furthermore, some couples refuse to interact face-to-face after particularly damaging messages are exchanged (Mitchell, 2010).

Conclusions

Personnel security measures are intended to prevent the loss of sensitive and valuable information, and loss can result either from the decisions of insiders to undermine this goal, or from the actions of hostile outside parties. Part I of this report introduced central cybersecurity concerns, with a primary focus on the social and cultural aspects of these risks. A great deal is known about external cyber threats, to include crime, terrorism, and counterintelligence. The necessary response is largely understood, and these topics have been addressed by other federal entities for some time. Part II outlined outside research on how changes to human behavior and society might affect the ability or willingness of insiders to protect information, but that the risks are not yet fully understood. The empirical studies conducted for this project, as summarized above, will together clarify cyberculture risks and potential ways for personnel security professionals to address and mitigate them.

The ultimate goal of the present project is to reach the point where personnel security policies, practices, and community awareness correspond to the psychological and cultural changes that have and are taking place. People today use computers to access more information, communicate more efficiently, and have more assistance than any generation in human history, so the impact is likely to be deep and have unexpected consequences. The first need is to raise awareness across the community about what can and does occur in cyberspace, ensure that the workforce is aware of how to responsibly and safely participate, and ensure that documents are updated to cover cyber activities that meet existing reporting requirements. The second need, and goal for moving forward, is to conduct research to establish fair and realistic coverage requirements for new topics, and to address situations where traditional assumptions about issues no longer make sense. Finally, because technology constantly evolves, new products and cultural changes must be periodically reviewed to ensure that personnel security activities are effective in protecting against the loss of controlled information.

References

AARP. (2010). Social media and technology use among adults 50+. Washington, DC: AARP.

Aboujaoude, E., Koran, L. M., Gamel, N., Large, M. D., & Serpe, R. T. (2006). Potential markers for problematic internet use: A telephone survey of 2,513 adults. CNS Spectrums, 11, 750-755.

Adams, W.L. (2008). UK couple to divorce over affair on Second Life. Time Magazine. Retrieved September 10, 2010, from http://www.time.com /time/world/article/0,8599,1859231,00.html.

Adjudicative Guidelines for Determining Eligibility for Access to Classified Information, December 29, 2005.

Ali, S. (2010). Small businesses join lawsuit against Yelp. Retrieved January 6, 2011, from http://blogs.wsj.com/digits/2010/03/17/small-businesses-join-lawsuit-against-yelp/

Albanesius, C. (2010). 'Call of Duty: Black Ops' Gamers Log 600M hours of play time. PCMAG.COM. Retrieved December 28, 2010, from http://www.pcmag.com/article2/0,2817,2374762,00.asp

American Heritage® Dictionary of the English language. (2010). Retrieved June 11, 2010, from http://education.yahoo.com/reference/dictionary/

American Psychiatric Association. (2000). Diagnostic and statistical manual of mental disorders (4th ed.). Washington, DC.

AmericasArmy.com (2010). America's Army Official Website. Retrieved June 7, 2010, from http://www.americasarmy.com/

Anderson, K. J. (2001). Internet use among college students: An exploratory study. Journal of American College Health, 50, 1, 21-26.

Armstrong, L., Phillips, J. G., & Saling, L. L. (2000). Potential determinants of heavier Internet usage. International Journal of Human-Computer Studies, 53, 537-550.

Barak, A. (2010). References related to the Internet & Psychology. Retrieved June 23, 2010, from http://construct.haifa.ac.il/~azy/refindx.htm

Bazelon, E. (2010). What really happened to Phoebe Prince? Slate Magazine. Retrieved July 30, 2010, from http://www.slate.com/id/2260952 /entry/2260953/

BBC News. (2005). South Korean dies after games session. Retrieved October 20, 2009, from http://news.bbc.co.uk/2/hi/technology/4137782.stm

BBC News. (2010). South Africa police hunt tweeting spy. Retrieved September 15, 2010, from http://www.bbc.co.uk/news/world-africa-11314555

Beard, K. W., & Wolf, E. M. (2001). Modification in the proposed diagnostic criteria for Internet addiction. Cyber Psychology and Behavior, 4, 377-383.

Bender, B. (2010). Pentagon workers tied to child porn. Retrieved July 30, 2010, from http://www.boston.com/news/nation/washington/articles/2010 /07/23/pe ntagon_workers_tied_to_child_porn/

Blair, D. (2010). Annual Threat Assessment of the US Intelligence Community for the Senate Select Committee on Intelligence, Denis C. Blair, Director of National Intelligence, February 2, 2010, 1-4. 111th Cong.

Black, D. W., Belsare, G., & Schlosser, S. (1999). Clinical features, psychiatric comorbidity, and health-related quality of life in persons reporting compulsive computer use behavior. The Journal of Clinical Psychiatry, 60, 839-844.

Block, J. J. (2008). Issues for DSM-IV: Internet addiction. The American Journal of Psychiatry, 165, 306-307.

Boutin, P. (2010). Mark Zuckerberg's personal mission: Convince the world to share. Retrieved June 8, 2010, from http://venturebeat.com/2010/05/20/facebook-privacy-mark-zuckerberg/

Brandon, J. (2007). The top eight corporate sites in Second Life. Retrieved June 9, 2010, from http://www.computerworld.com/s/article/9018238/The_top_eight_corporat e_sites_in_Second_Life

Brodkin, J. (2008). IBM, Second Life create business-friendly virtual worlds. Retrieved June 9, 2010, from http://www.networkworld.com/news/2008/040308-ibm-second-lifevirtual.html

Bush, R. (2009). Reynard proposers' day IARPA-BAA-09-05 overview. Retrieved July 31, 2009, from http://www.iarpa.gov/Reynard_Proposers_Day_Overview.pdf

Businessweek. (2006). My virtual life. Business Week. Retrieved June 9, 2010, from http://www.businessweek.com/magazine/content/06_18/b3982001.htm

Caplan, S. E. (2002). Problematic internet use and psychosocial well-being: Development of a theory-based cognitive-behavioral measurement instrument. Computers in Human Behavior, 18, 553-575.

Caplan, S. E., Williams, D., & Yee, N. (2009). Problematic internet use and psychosocial well-being among MMO players. Computers in Human Behavior, 25, 1312-1319.

Carnagey, N. L., Anderson, C. A., & Bushman, B. J. (2007). The effect of video game violence on physiological desensitization to real-life violence. Journal of Experimental Social Psychology, 43, 489-496.

Carton, B. (2010). 'I Can Stalk U': A 'Please Rob Me' for people who upload photos to Twitter. Retrieved September 15, 2010, from http://legalblogwatch.typepad.com/legal_blog_watch/2010/09/i-can-stalk-u-a-please-rob-me-for-people-who-upload-photos-to-twitter.html

Caspi, A., & Gorsky, P. (2006). Online deception: Prevalence, motivation, and emotion. Cyber Psychology and Behavior, 9, 54-59.

Cavaglion, G. (2008). Voices of coping in an Italian self-help virtual community of cyberporn dependents. Cyber Psychology and Behavior, 11, 599-601.

Chabinsky, S. R. (2009). Statement of Steven R. Chabinsky Deputy Assistant Director, Cyber Division, Federal Bureau of Investigation before the

Senate Judiciary Committee Subcommittee on Terrorism and Homeland Security at a hearing entitled "Cybersecurity: Preventing Terrorist Attacks and Protecting Privacy Rights in Cyberspace." Presented November 17, 2009, 1- 6, 111th Cong.

Chang, D. (2010). Augmented reality meets Facebook. Retrieved May 17, 2010, from http://asia.cnet.com/crave/2010/02/21/augmented-reality-meets-socialnetworking/

Chappell, D., Eatough, V., Davies, M. N. O., & Griffiths, M. (2006). EverQuest – It's just a computer game right? An interpretative phenomenological analysis of online gaming addiction. International Journal of Mental Health and Addiction, 4, 205-216.

Chen, S. (2009). The social network game boom. Retrieved August 2, 2010, from http://www.gamasutra.com/view/feature/4009/the_social_network_game_ boom.php

Clark, D. (2010). Second Life creator Linden Lab downsizes, morphs. Retrieved September 6, 2010, from http://blogs.wsj.com/digits /2010/06/10/secondlife-creator-linden-lab-downsizes-morphs/

CNN. (2009). Text messages of engineer in deadly train wreck detailed. Retrieved December 22, 2010, from http://articles.cnn.com/2009-03-05/us/train.text_1_union-pacific-freight-train-locomotive-cell-phone?_s=PM:US

Cohen, S., Doyle, W. J., Skoner, D. P., Rabin, B. S., & Gwaltney, J. M. (1997). Social ties and susceptibility to the common cold. Journal of the American Medical Association, 277, 1940-1944.

Collins, L. (2008). Friend game: Behind the online hoax that led to a girl's suicide. New Yorker. Retrieved July 30, 2010, from http://www.newyorker.com/reporting/2008/01/21/080121fa_fact_collins?currentPage=all

Corbett, P. (2010). Facebook demographics and statistics report June 2010 – Privacy concerns don't stop growth. Retrieved December 22, 2010, from http://www.istrategylabs.com/2010/06/facebook-demographics-and-statistics-report-june-2010-%E2%80%93-privacy-concerns-dont-stop-growth/

Davis, R. A. (2001). A cognitive-behavioral model of pathological Internet use (PIU). Computers in Human Behavior, 17, 187-195.

Davis, R. A., Flett, G. L., & Besser, A. (2002). Validation of a new scale for measuring problematic internet use: Implications for pre-employment screening. Cyber Psychology and Behavior, 5, 331-345.

Department of Defense. (2006, June). Nuclear Weapons Personnel Reliability Program (PRP) Regulation. Washington, DC: Author.

Diana, A. (2010). Air Force Warns Against Location Based Sites. Retrieved March 9, 2011, from http://www.informationweek.com/news/government /mobile/showArticle.jhtml?articleID=228300144&cid=RSSfeed_IWK_ All

Dill, K. E., & Dill, J.C. (1998). Video game violence: A review of the empirical literature. Aggression and Violent Behavior, 3, 407-428

Ducheneaut, N., Yee, N., Nickell, E., & Moore, R. J. (2006). Building an MMO with mass appeal: A look at gameplay in World of Warcraft. Games and Culture, 1, 281-317.

El Gazzar, S., Vitorovich, L., & Bender, R. (2011). 3rd UPDATE: Egypt Communications Cut As Protests Continue. Wall Street Journal. Retrieved January 28, 2011, from http://online.wsj.com/article/BT-CO-20110128-709816.html

Elgan, M. (2010). Are you a social networking mutant? Retrieved June 7, 2010, from http://www.computerworld.com/s/article/9177694/Are_you_ a_social_netw orking_mutant_?

Executive Order 12968, Access to Classified Information, August 7, 1995.

Flaherty, A. (2009, February 12). Congressman's online Twitter posts raise security concerns. Boston Globe. Retrieved September 10, 2009, from http://www.boston.com/news/nation/washington/articles/2009/02/12/co ngressmans_online_twitter_posts_raise_security_concerns/

Fox News. (2006). Chinese "Warcraft" game distributor sued over teen's suicide. Retrieved October 8, 2009, from http://www.foxnews.com /story/0,2933,195236,00.html

Fox News. (2007). Boy collapses after playing "World of Warcraft" for 24 hours. Retrieved October 8, 2009, from http://www.foxnews.com/story /0,2933,453447,00.html

Fox News. (2008). Online game meetings sometimes end tragically, but phenomenon remains rare. Retrieved October 9, 2009, from http://www.foxnews.com/story/0,2933,316333,00.html

Francescani, C., & Kucharz, C. (2007). Virtual child porn riles law enforcement. Retrieved July 29, 2010, from http://abcnews.go.com/The Law/story?id=3159871

Frontline. (2009). Taking out the Taliban; Home for dinner. Retrieved June 7, 2010, from http://www.pbs.org/wgbh/pages/frontline/digitalnation /wagingwar/remote-control-war/taking-out-the-taliban-home-for-dinner.html

Gentile, D. A., Lynch, P. J., Linder, J. R., & Walsh, D. A. (2004). The effects of violent video game habits on adolescent hostility, aggressive behaviors, and school performance. Journal of Adolescence, 27, 5-22.

Google. (2010). Retrieved May 17, 2010, from http://www.google.com /mobile/goggles/#landmark

Greenfield, D. N., & Davis, R. A. (2002). Lost in cyberspace: The web @ work. Cyber Psychology and Behavior, 5, 347-353.

Gross, D. (2010). The Facebook games that millions love (and hate). Retrieved August 2, 2010, from http://www.cnn.com/2010/TECH/02/23/facebook. games/index.html

Hachman, M. (2010). f8: Facebook touts 'Open Graph,' Connects with smaller sites. PCMAG.COM. Retrieved June 16, 2010, from http://www.pcmag.com/article2/0,2817,2362920,00.asp

Hawkley, L. C., Thisted, R. A., & Cacioppo, J. T. (2009). Loneliness predicts reduced physical activity: Cross-sectional & longitudinal analyses. Health Psychology, 28, 354-363.

Henthorn, D. (2010). Ohio state flash mob goes viral: Link to video. Retrieved May 18, 2010, from http://www.associatedcontent.com/article/2973592 /ohio_state_flash_mob_ goes_viral_link.html?cat=7

Herbig, K. L. (2008). Changes in espionage by Americans: 1947-2007. Monterey, CA: Defense Personnel Security Research Center.

Hersh, S. M. (2004). Torture at Abu Ghraib. The New Yorker. Retrieved September 6, 2010, from http://www.newyorker.com/archive/2004/05/10 /040510fa_fact

Hopkins. C. (2010). Second Life economy at record high. Retrieved June 11, 2010, from http://www.readwriteweb.com/archives/second_life_econo my_at_record_hig h.php

IACP. (2010). Developing a Cybervetting Strategy for Law Enforcement. Alexandria, VA: International Association of Chiefs of Police.

Immordino-Yang, M. H., McColl, A., Damasio, H., & Damasio, A. (2009). Neural correlates of admiration and compassion. Proceedings of the National Academy of Sciences, 106, 8021-8026.

Ionescu, D. (2010). Geolocation 101: How it works, the apps, and your privacy. PC World. Retrieved May 17, 2010, from http://www.pcworld. com/article/192803/geolo.html?tk=rss_news

Ivory, J. D., & Kalyanaraman, S. (2007). The effects of technological advancement and violent content in video games on players' feelings of presence, involvement, physiological arousal, and aggression. Journal of Communication, 57, 532-555.

Kelkar, K. (2010). Flash mobs flood the city on Valentine's Day. Retrieved May 17, 2010, from http://www.sfexaminer.com/local/Flash-mobs-flood-The-Cityon-Valentines-day-84356747.html

Kim, J., LaRose, R., & Peng, W. (2009). Loneliness as the cause and the effect of problematic Internet use: The relationships between Internet use and psychological well being. Cyber Psychology and Behavior, 12, 451-455.

King, S. A. (1999). Internet gambling and pornography: Illustrative examples of the psychological consequences of communication anarchy. Cyber Psychology and Behavior, 2, 175-184.

Kirkpatrick, M. (2006). Metaverse breached: Second Life customer database hacked. Retrieved January 11, 2011, from http://techcrunch.com/2006/09 /08/metaverse-breached-second-lifecustomer-database-hacked/

Kirkpatrick, M. (2010). Facebook's Zuckerberg says the age of privacy is over. Retrieved May 17, 2010, from http://www.readwriteweb.com/archives /facebooks_zuckerberg_says_the_ag e_of_privacy_is_ov.php

Konijn, E. A., Bijvank, M. N., & Bushman, B. J. (2007). I wish I were a warrior: The role of wishful identification in the effects of violent video games on aggression in adolescent boys. Developmental Psychology, 43, 1038-1044.

Kraut, R., Patterson, M., Lundmark, V., Kiesler, S., Mukopadhyay, T., & Scherlis, W. (1998). Internet paradox: A social technology that reduces social involvement and psychological well-being? American Psychologist, 53, 1017- 1031.

Leung, L. (2002). Loneliness, self-disclosure, and ICQ ("I Seek You") use. Cyber Psychology and Behavior, 5, 241-251.

Li, Q. (2006). Cyberbullying in schools: A research of gender differences. School Psychology International, 27, 157-170.

Li, Q. (2007). New bottle but old wine: A research of cyberbullying in schools. Computers in Human Behavior, 23, 1777-1791.

Linden Lab. (2008). Second life virtual economy demographic summary information

through November 2008. Retrieved August 3, 2009, from http://static-secondlife-com.s3.amazonaws.com/economy/stats_200811.xls

Lipowicz, A. (2010). vGov for feds aims to be a more engaging online environment. Retrieved July 27, 2010, from http://fcw.com/articles /2010/07/12/featqanda-paulette-robinson-ndu-vgov.aspx?sc_lang=en

Lund, R., Christensen, U., Holstein, B. E., Due, P, & Osler, M. (2006). Influence of marital history over two and three generations on early death.

A longitudinal study of Danish men born in 1953. Journal of Epidemiology and Community Health, 60, 496-501.

Mafiawarstips.com (2010). The basics of Mafia wars. Retrieved May 18, 2010, from www.mafiawarstips.com/Guide/TheBasics.html

Maldives Mission (2010). Maldives virtual embassy. Retrieved September 3, 2010, from http://maldivesmission.ch/index.php?id=65

Marines. (2009). Immediate ban of internet social networking sites (SNS) on Marine Corps enterprise network (MCEN) NIPRNET. Retrieved January 20, 2011, from http://www.marines.mil/news/messages/pages/maradmin 0458- 09.aspx

Marines. (2010). Responsible and effective use of internet-based capabilities. Retrieved January 20, 2011, from http://www.marines.mil/news /messages/Pages/MARADMIN181-10.aspx

McKeon, M. (2010). The evolution of privacy on Facebook. Retrieved August 2, 2010, from http://mattmckeon.com/facebook-privacy/

McKenna, K. Y. A., & Bargh, J. A. (2000). Plan 9 from cyberspace: The implications of the internet for personality and social psychology. Personality and Social Psychology Review, 4, 57-75.

McMillan, R. (2011). Man used Facebook to try to blackmail girl for porn. PC World. Retrieved February 4, 2011, from http://www.pcworld.com /article/218582/Man_Used_Facebook_to_Try_to_Bl ackmail_Girl_for_Porn.html?tk=rss_news

Meerkerk, G. J. (2007). Pwned by the internet: Explorative research into the causes and consequences of compulsive internet use. Rotterdam: IVO.

Mehdizadeh, S. (2010). Self-presentation 2.0: Narcissism and self-esteem on Facebook. Cyberpsychology, Behavior, and Social Networking, 13, 357-364.

Mitchell, R. L. (2010). Cop: Texting plays rising role in domestic disturbances. Retrieved September 15, 2010, from http://blogs.computerworld.com/16940/cop_texting_plays_rising_role_in_d omestic_disturbances

Morahan-Martin, J., & Schumacher, P. (2000). Incidence and correlates of pathological Internet use among college students. Computer in Human Behavior, 16, 13-29.

Morrison, C. M., & Gore, H. (2010). The relationship between excessive Internet use and depression: A questionnaire-based study of 1,319 young people and adults. Psychopathology, 43, 121-126.

MSNBC.com. (2007). Hey parents, leave online gaming to the kids. Retrieved November 9, 2009, from http://today.msnbc.msn.com/id/19855372 /ns/technology_and_sciencetech_and_gadgets

Nalwa, K., & Anand, A. P. (2003). Internet addiction in students: A cause of concern. Cyber Psychology and Behavior, 6, 653-656.

NCIS. (2010). Cyber. Retrieved December 17, 2010, from http://www.ncis.navy.mil/CoreMissions/cyber/Pages/default.aspx

Ng, B. D., & Wiemer-Hastings, P. (2005). Addiction to the internet and online gaming. Cyber Psychology and Behavior, 8, 110-114.

The Nielsen Company. (2010). Social networks/blogs now account for one in every four and a half minutes online. Retrieved July 6, 2010, from http://blog.nielsen.com/nielsenwire/online_mobile/social-media-accounts-for-22-percent-of-time-online/

Nino, T. (2010). Second Life statistical charts. Retrieved June 11, 2010, from http://dwellonit.taterunino.net/sl-statistical-charts/

O'Reilly, K. (2004). Ethnographic methods. New York, NY: Routledge.

Padilla-Walker, L. M., Nelson, L. J., Carroll, J. S., & Jensen, A. C. (2009). More than a just a game: Video game and internet use during emerging adulthood. Journal of Youth and Adolescence. Retrieved October 30, 2009, from http://www.springerlink.com/content/w487673k5415k142 /fulltext.pdf

Parrish, K. (2010). Blizzard cracks down erotic role-playing in WoW. Retrieved December 13, 2010, from http://www.tomshardware. com/news/World-ofWarcraft-MMO-MMORPG,11020.html

Paul, I. (2010). The Facebook data torrent debacle: Q&A. PC World. Retrieved August 2, 2010, from http://www.pcworld.com /article/202167 /The_Facebook_Data_Torrent_Dow nload_QA.html?tk=rss_news

Pew Research Center (2010). Older adults and social media: Social networking use among those ages 50 and older nearly doubled over the past year. Retrieved September 6, 2010, from http://pewinternet.org /Reports/2010/OlderAdults-and-Social-Media.aspx

Reuters. (2007). UPDATE 3 - Linden Lab outlaws Second Life gambling. Retrieved June 9, 2010, from http://secondlife.reuters.com/stories/2007 /07/26/linden-lab-outlawssecond-life-gambling/

Reuters. (2008). Ageplay sim eyes new grid. Retrieved June 10, 2010, from http://secondlife.reuters.com/stories/2008/03/11/ageplay-sim-eyes-new-grid/index.html

Rideout, V. J., Foehr, U. G., & Roberts, D. F. (2010). Generation M2: Media in the lives of 8- to 18-year-olds. Retrieved September 6, 2010, from http://www.kff.org/entmedia/8010.cfm

Riley, D. (2007). You're not in the USSR any more: Estonia opens an embassy in Second Life. Retrieved July 14, 2010, from http://techcrunch.com/2007 /12/05/youre-not-in-the-ussr-any-moreestonia-opens-an-embassy-in-second-life/

Rinckey, G. (2009). Commentary: Social sites risk security clearance. Retrieved November 17, 2009, from http://federaltimes.va. newsmemory.com

Riva, G. (2002). The sociocognitive psychology of computer-mediated communication: The present and future of technology-based interactions. CyberPsychology & Behavior, 5, 581-598.

Rosenwald, M. S. (2010). Second Life's virtual money can become real-life cash.

Retrieved July 29, 2010, from http://www.washingtonpost.com/wp-dyn/content/article/2010/03/07/AR2010030703524.html?hpid=topnews

Semuels, A. (2007). Virtual marketers have second thoughts about Second Life. Retrieved June 9, 2010, from http://articles.latimes.com /2007/jul/14/business/fi-secondlife14

Shapira, N. A., Goldsmith, T. D., Keck, P. E., Khosla, U. M., & McElroy, S. L. (2000). Psychiatric features of individuals with problematic internet use. Journal of Affective Disorders 57, 267–272.

Shapira, N. A., Lessig, M. C., Goldsmith, T. D., Szabo, S. T., Lazoritz, M., Gold, M. S., et al. (2003). Problematic internet use: Proposed classification and diagnostic criteria. Depression and Anxiety, 17, 207-216.

Sheridan, M. (2010). 100 teens turn snowball fight into violent flash mob outside Philadelphia Macy's store. Retrieved May 17, 2010, from http://www.nydailynews.com/news/national/2010/02/17/2010-02-17_100_teens_turn_snowball_fight_into_violent_flash_mob_outside_phil adelp hia_macys.html

Sigman, A. (2009). Well connected? The biological implications of "social networking." Biologist, 56, 14-20.

Simmons, C. (2007). Sweden opens virtual embassy 3D-style. Retrieved September 3, 2010, from http://www.sweden.se/eng/Home/Lifestyle /Reading/Second-Life/

Slatalla, M. (2009). Caught in the deceit of the web. Retrieved September 6, 2010, from http://www.nytimes.com/2009/08/13/fashion/13spy.html.

Smith, A. (2010). Mobile access 2010. Retrieved July 7, 2010, from http://www.pewinternet.org/Reports/2010/Mobile-Access-2010.aspx

Smith, J.R. (2010). Would you want a digital footprint from birth? Retrieved October 7, 2010, from http://jrsmith.blog.avg.com/2010/10/would-you-want-adigital-footprint-from-birth.html

Smith, P., Mahdavi, J., Carvalho, M., & Tippett, N. (2006, July). An investigation into cyberbullying, its forms, awareness and impact, and the relationship between age and gender in cyberbullying. Research Brief, Brief No: RBX03- 06.

Snow, G. (2010). Statement before the House Judiciary Subcommittee on Crime, Terrorism, and Homeland Security Washington, D.C. Retrieved December 17, 2010, from http://www.fbi.gov/news/testimony/the-fbi2019s-efforts-tocombat-cyber-crime-on-social-networking-sites

Steel, E. (2010). A web pioneer profiles users by name. Wall Street Journal. Retrieved January 11, 2011, from http://online.wsj.com/article/SB10001 424052702304410504575560243259416072.html

Steinberg, S. (2010). Apple game center: The Facebook of mobile gaming? Retrieved July 6, 2010, from http://www.cnn.com/2010/TECH /gaming.gadgets/07/05/apple.game.cen ter.steinberg/index.html

Stone, B. (2010). The children of cyberspace: Old fogies by their 20s. Retrieved June 3, 2010, from http://www.nytimes.com/2010/01/10/week inreview/10stone.html?scp=1&sq=technology%20generation%20gap& st=cse

Subrahmanyam, K., & Greenfield, P. (2008, Spring). Online communication and adolescent relationships. The Future of Children, 18, 119-146. Retrieved June 21, 2010, from http://www.jstor.org/stable/20053122

Suler, J. (2004). The online disinhibition effect. Cyber Psychology and Behavior, 7, 321-326.

Sussman, B. (2007). Teachers, college students lead a Second Life. Retrieved June 9, 2010, from http://www.usatoday.com/news/education/2007-08-01-second-life_N.htm

Terdiman, D. (2006). Phony kids, virtual sex. Retrieved August 5, 2009, from http://news.cnet.com/Phony-kids,-virtual-sex/2100-1043_3-6060132.html

Terdiman, D. (2008). Banks banned in 'Second Life.' Retrieved June 9, 2010, from http://news.cnet.com/8301-13772_3-9845886-52.html?tag=mncol;txt

Timpane, J. (2011). Arab world shaken by the power of Twitter and Facebook. Retrieved January 28, 2011, from http://articles.philly.com/2011-01-27/news/27051558_1_social-media-facebook-page-twitter-and-facebook

VNUnet News. (2002). Second gamer dies after massive binge. Retrieved October 6, 2009, from http://www.v3.co.uk/vnunet/news/2120472/second-gamerdies-massive-binge

Waterman, S. (2010). Fictitious femme fatale fooled cybersecurity. Retrieved July 28, 2010, from http://www.washingtontimes.com/news /2010/jul/18/fictitiousfemme-fatale-fooled-cybersecurity/

Weaver, J. B., Mays, D., Weaver, S. S., Kannenberg, W., Hopkins, G. L., Eroglu, D., & Bernhardt, J. M. (2009). Health-risk correlates of video-game playing among adults. American Journal of Preventative Medicine, 37, 299-305.

White, J. (2005). It's a video game, and an Army recruiter. Retrieved June 7, 2010, from http://www.washingtonpost.com/wpdyn/content/article/2005 /05/26/AR2005052601505.html

Williams, D., Yee, N., & Caplan, S. E. (2008). Who plays, how much, and why? A behavioral player census of virtual world. Journal of Computer-Mediated Communication, 13, 993-1018.

Woollacott, E. (2010). Second Life to become browser-based as Linden Lab restructures. Retrieved June 10, 2010, from http://www.tgdaily.com /games-and-entertainment-features/50158-second-life-to-become-browser-based-as-linden-restructures

Yee, N. (2004). The Daedalus gateway: The psychology of MMORPGs. Retrieved June 8, 2010, from http://www.nickyee.com/daedalus /gateway_addiction.html

Young, J. (2010). After frustrations in Second Life, colleges look to new virtual worlds. Retrieved June 9, 2010, from http://chronicle.com/article /AfterFrustrations-in-Second/64137/

Young, K. S. (1998). Internet addiction: The emergence of a new clinical disorder. Cyber Psychology and Behavior, 1, 237-244.

Young, K. S. (2008). Internet sex addiction risk factors, stages of development, and treatment. American Behavioral Scientist, 52, 21-37.

Young K. S., & Rogers, R. C. (1998). The relationship between depression and Internet addiction. Cyber Psychology and Behavior, 1, 25-28.

Zani, D. (2010). Lightsaber flash mob attacks an innocent shopping mall. Retrieved May 17, 2010, from http://www.cinemablend.com /new/Lightsaber-FlashMob-Attacks-An-Innocent-Shopping-Mall-17095.html

Zavis, A. (2009). Judge tentatively dismisses case in MySpace hoax that led to teenage girl's suicide. Retrieved July 30, 2010, from http://latimesblogs.latimes.com/lanow/2009/07/myspace-sentencing.html

Zhao, S., Grasmuck, S., & Martin, J. (2008). Identity construction on Facebook: Digital empowerment in anchored relationships. Computers in Human Behavior, 24, 1816-1836.

End Notes

[1] It is possible to create independent or fictitious profiles on many social networks, such as for privacy when engaging in activities that may be criticized, keeping circles of associates apart, manipulation or social engineering, etc.

[2] The present research is concerned with personnel security, as general information on cyberculture is available from numerous other sources. For example, Barak (2010) maintains a website dedicated to cataloging research on psychology and the internet conducted since 1996. It includes sections on research about children, the elderly, addiction and crime, gaming and gambling, virtual communities, and many other topics.

In: Cyberculture and the Potential Effects ... ISBN: 978-1-63117-964-8
Editor: Walter P. Barnes

Chapter 2

CYBER CULTURE AND PERSONNEL SECURITY: REPORT II – ETHNOGRAPHIC ANALYSIS OF SECOND LIFE*

Olga G. Shechter, Eric L. Lang and Christina R. Keibler

BACKGROUND

This report presents an ethnographic analysis of a popular virtual social environment, Second Life, as the second part of a larger effort to study the impact of involvement in cyberculture on personnel security and safety outcomes. Research has shown that traits and behaviors that individuals take on online can spill over into their offline lives, which could be of concern to the extent that their online behavior demonstrates poor judgment and/or undermines their reliability. The current personnel security vetting process focuses on behaviors that occur in the real world, without explicitly addressing how cyber world activities can be associated with many national security concerns. The present study contains implications for how to address the risks stemming from problematic cyber involvement during investigative, adjudicative, and continuing evaluation phases.

* This is an edited, reformatted and augmented version of Technical Report 11-03, issued by The Defense Personnel and Security Research Center (PERSEREC), dated July 2011.

Abstract

This report presents the results from an ethnographic examination of a popular virtual social environment, Second Life, as the second part of a larger effort to study the impact of participation in cyber activities on personnel security and safety. Research has shown that cyber participation can spill over into individuals' offline lives, which could be of security concern to the extent that their online behavior demonstrates poor judgment and/or undermines their reliability. Several immersive ethnographic methods were used in the present study, including participation observation, group discussions, and one-on-one interviews with 148 Second Life users who resembled the demographics of clearance holders.

The reported findings include a description of behaviors of potential concern, a set of case studies that outline the behaviors of actual users, and a framework of user personas that attempts to distinguish between innocuous use of no apparent security concern from problematic use that may pose risks to national security. These findings contain implications for updating personnel security policy regarding cyber involvement.

Executive Summary

Project Overview

This report represents the second part of a larger effort to understand the effects of active involvement in cyberculture on workplace behavior, reliability, security, and personnel safety. Cyberculture involves the use and increased reliance on computer networks for communication, entertainment, work, and business and has a very strong presence in today's society. Although the impact of cyberculture on outcomes of personnel security has not been examined before empirically, research has shown that behaviors and personality traits that individuals take on in cyberspace can spill over and affect their behavior in the brick-and mortar-world, and ultimately, their conduct in the workplace.

The first part of this effort, Report I, set the stage for the Cyber Culture and Personnel Security Project, outlined reasons for concern, and described presently actionable findings and strategies.

The present report provides results from an ethnographic investigation of the virtual social environment, Second Life, including behaviors of security concern that occur there and a typology for distinguishing between innocuous and problematic user participation. Future research will (1) use quantitative survey methods to assess how frequently behaviors of security concern actually occur in actual in potential clearance holders and whether these behaviors are associated with reduced judgment, reliability, and trustworthiness in the workplace, and (2) make actionable recommendations for how to address the risks stemming from problematic cyber participation during investigative, adjudicative, and continuing evaluation phases.

Project Goals and Methods

The present study of Second Life was conducted in collaboration with two contracted research staff with expertise in ethnographic research methods and virtual worlds. The primary goals of this work were to:

1) Describe behaviors of personnel security concern that individuals exhibit in Second Life using the Adjudicative Guidelines for Determining the Eligibility for Access to Classified Information as a framework.
2) Describe the nature, breadth, and severity of real-life behavioral consequences, i.e., "spillover," resulting from involvement in Second Life.
3) Develop an initial typology framework for distinguishing between innocuous and problematic forms of participation in Second Life.

Immersive ethnographic methods were used to directly interview 68 Second Life users both inside this virtual environment and in real life regarding their participation and its impact on their lives. The researchers interviewed another 80 respondents indirectly or through informal discussion groups. They also logged approximately 800 hours of participant observation and observation data collection time.

All efforts were made to ensure that interviewed respondents were similar to actual clearance holders in respect to vital demographics.

Findings

Behaviors of Personnel Security Concern

A number of behaviors observed and reported by participants in Second Life raised security concerns about the judgment, reliability, and trustworthiness of individuals who participate in them. Not all of these behaviors dealt with personnel security outcomes, and a number of them concerned broader suitability issues, as well as health-related concerns which could affect personnel's ability to perform their day-to-day work tasks. These health-related issues are particularly salient for personnel who occupy sensitive positions with additional requirements (e.g., DoD's Personnel Reliability Program positions). The identified behaviors can be grouped into four categories, which are described below:

Behaviors That Can be Used to Negatively Influence Personnel

A core concern for personnel security is that individuals might become targets for blackmail or influence by foreign or domestic agents who are trying to gather intelligence about the United States. In many cases, it only takes a small amount of detective work to figure out Second Life users' real-life identities, which can be pieced together from chats with them, user profiles, and information available via the web (e.g., search engines, social media and professional websites, etc.). The bulk of these behaviors concerns sexual and criminal activities, but they also include contact with foreign individuals or organizations and associations with extremist groups, which could open up avenues for foreign and ideological influence. Although behaviors in this category are limited to the virtual realm and lack direct physical contact, they can make individuals just as vulnerable to blackmail as real-world behaviors. Also, sometimes the behaviors listed below can translate into real-life encounters.

Behaviors That Compromise Performance and Reliability in the Workplace

Behaviors in this category concern the relationship between participation in Second Life and workplace performance and reliability. Individuals who spend excessive time in-world also reported having a poor sleep schedule, skipping work, having a difficult time focusing on work tasks, and even attempting to access Second Life while at work. These behaviors would be a security risk for jobs demanding a superior ability to sustain cognitive focus on tasks (e.g., working with nuclear materials or weapons).

This category also includes behaviors that involve illegal computer activities and violations of personal conduct in Second Life. It is plausible that individuals who abuse Second Life's Information Technology (IT) infrastructure in-world would also have a difficult time complying with IT rules and regulations in the workplace.

Behaviors That Undermine Mental and Physical Health

Disturbed mental health could cause a significant deficit to an individual's psychological, social and occupational functioning. Compulsive cyber use surfaced as one of the most prominent concerns in this category. This condition is behaviorally similar to other forms of addiction (e.g., alcohol, drugs, etc.), and in the present context involves such features as excessive use of Second Life, withdrawal symptoms when the Second Life access is inaccessible, build-up of tolerance including the need for more hours in-world, and negative social and occupational consequences. It cannot be concluded that the participants in the present study met the clinical criteria for compulsive cyber use, but they exhibited the symptoms of this condition. This category also includes behaviors associated with undermined physical health. While not a security risk, poor physical health may be a safety risk for all personnel, and particularly, those who occupy positions affording assess to certain critical materials, (i.e., nuclear materials, biological select agents, etc.)

Behaviors That Interfere with Real-World Functioning and Relationships

Many behaviors that exist in Second Life may not directly affect work performance or health-related quality of life, but they can negatively affect users' functioning in the brick-and-mortar world and their relationships with friends, coworkers, and family members.

Findings from the present study show that problematic Second Life involvement can break up relationships and marriages and result in neglect of spouses, children, and friends. It is of potential concern that over time some individuals may start replacing their real-world connections with virtual connections and fully disconnect from society. Their real-life emotional safety net may diminish in favor of one that exists in cyber space. Behaviors in this category therefore focus on consequences of problematic Second Life use on real-world functioning and relationships.

Case Studies

A set of case studies was developed on the basis of extensive one-on-one interviews with a subset of the participants. These case studies provide insight into the impact of Second Life involvement on respondents' real-world functioning, relationships, work life, mental health, and physical health. They suggest that we may be able to determine whether personnel are engaged in innocuous versus problematic use based on the functional role that Second Life plays in their life. The three functional roles that were identified included: (1) using Second Life as a tool for enhancing real life, (2) using Second Life as a temporary escape from real life, and (3) using Second Life as a replacement for real life.

Personas

The present ethnography identified five original personas that best capture and describe the wide range of Second Life users: Reckless Risk Takers, Escapists, Substitutes, Explorers, and Enhancers. Reckless Risk Takers use Second Life to partake in risky behaviors, both in terms of the potential harm of these behaviors to their own health and functioning, and the potential damage to their image if others find out about these behaviors. Escapists use Second Life to avoid their real-life problems. They neglect themselves, their families, and jobs and use Second Life much like a functional alcoholic uses alcohol. Substitutes use Second Life in place of television, hobbies, or even participation in nonmainstream sexual activities that may be difficult to satisfy in real life. Explorers use Second Life as a tool for discovering new places and experiences that are not readily accessible in real life. Finally, Enhancers fall into the group that is of least concern and seemingly the least frequently encountered in Second Life. They use Second Life as a tool for being more productive in real life.

Implications and Initial Recommendations

The present ethnography contains implications for revising the personnel security vetting and continuous evaluation process in three important ways.

1) **Update Definition of Contact in Adjudicative Guidelines.** The national Adjudicative Guidelines currently focus exclusively on behaviors that occur in the real world, without recognizing that the cyber world involves activities associated with nearly all of the concerns described in the guidelines.
   The lives that individuals build and lead in virtual worlds such as Second Life have very real consequences for their health, job performance, and real-world functioning. It is time to reevaluate and expand the definitions of contact, outside experience and activities for the purposes of defining a behavior as potentially adverse, and also update both the investigative standards and the adjudicative guidelines to reflect the changing security risks resulting from involvement in virtual realities.
2) **Educate Personnel How to Avoid Risks.** The present findings can educate personnel who desire to participate in virtual realities but do not understand the potential risks for the workplace and real-life functioning.
   Personnel education can be accomplished by providing informational materials or developing an online training module on the potential risks to performance in the workplace, physical and mental health, and real-life functioning.
   The training materials should also provide strategies for how to avoid these risks and participate in virtual realities in a safe and productive manner.
3) **Implement Peer Reporting Systems.** Problematic cyber involvement may be difficult to detect through self-reports or automated checks, so peer reporting may play a vital role in its identification. Personnel should therefore be taught how to distinguish signs of problematic cyber use from routine or healthy cyber involvement in their colleagues and how to appropriately report these indicators. Previous research has shown that employees are reluctant to report coworker behavior that isn't directly associated with national security, and without adequate education, cyber use may fall into this category. Personnel education will therefore be a crucial first step before peer reporting can be successfully implemented.

INTRODUCTION

Project Description

This report describes the findings from an ethnographic investigation of the virtual social environment, Second Life. It is the second part of the Defense Personnel Security Research Center's (PERSEREC) larger effort to investigate the effects of active involvement in cyber activities on outcomes of high relevance to national security, i.e., workplace behavior, reliability, security, and personnel safety. The first report set the stage by outlining the goals of the project, presenting an overview of how broader cyber security issues interact with the interests of personnel security, and summarizing a wide range of literature on the potential consequences participation in cyber environments. Building on the first two projects, additional planned research will assess how frequently clearance holders participate in cyber behaviors of potential security concern, and provide specific recommendations on cyber environments for policy makers, investigators, and adjudicators. This work is distinct from a separate PERSEREC research effort that is seeking to determine appropriate policies and practices for vetting cyber behavior of subjects who are under consideration for new or continued national security positions (IACP, 2010). Taken together, these projects support PERSEREC's mission of strengthening Department of Defense's (DoD) personnel security clearance system by evaluating new threats introduced by cyber participation.

Ethnographies are a popular tool for exploring unknown cultures, and although they have been used to study Second Life in the past (e.g., Boellstorff, 2008), none have examined this cyber environment in the context of potential personnel security risks. The ethnographic method involves examining the cultural norms, perspectives, and characteristics of the culture in question through extensive observations and interviews, and then formulating descriptive statements about the lives of its natives. This approach was chosen in lieu of a more quantitative survey method due to its appropriateness for the study of new cultures. It was reasoned that once a qualitative description of potential risks endemic to Second Life and other cyber environments is established, survey methods can be used, as the next step, to understand how prevalent these behaviors are in clearance holders.

The present study of Second Life had three main goals:

1) Describe behaviors of personnel security concern that individuals exhibit in Second Life using the Adjudicative Guidelines for

Determining the Eligibility for Access to Classified Information as a framework.

2) Describe the nature, breadth, and severity of real-life behavioral consequences, i.e., "spillover," resulting from involvement in Second Life.
3) Develop an initial typology framework for distinguishing between innocuous and problematic forms of participation in Second Life.

The Adjudicative Guidelines

The Adjudicative Guidelines for Determining the Eligibility for Access to Classified Information, which will be referred to as Adjudicative Guidelines from here on, are the guiding framework for understanding behaviors of security concern considered during investigations, adjudications, and adverse actions (e.g., the approval or revocation of a clearance). The Adjudicative Guidelines apply to any United States government personnel or contractors requiring access to classified information. They include 13 criteria that are considered during the adjudicative process, which is an examination of a person of interest's life in sufficient duration and depth to understand the nuances of their behaviors, both positive and negative, and make a decision regarding that individual's continued or pending access to classified information.

Second Life is a virtual social environment that parallels the real world in many respects, and so it can be a new context for behaviors of potential concern described in the Adjudicative Guidelines. The only key difference is that virtual environments lack the physical contact present in real life. In order to maximize the relevance of this research to the needs of personnel security community, the researchers decided to use the guidelines as a framework for understanding security risk in Second Life and organizing study results. Paraphrased descriptions of the 13 guidelines are provided below:

- **Guideline A: Allegiance to the United States**. An individual must have unquestioned allegiance to the United States. Allegiance is compromised when an individual uses force or violence in seeking to overthrow or influence the United States government, prevent others from exercising their constitutional rights, or deliberately harm the United States. Actions that could harm United States national security include espionage, sabotage, sedition, terrorism, and treason.

- **Guideline B: Foreign Influence**. An individual's foreign family members or other individuals to whom he or she is bound by affection should not create the potential for foreign influence. Foreign contacts may be a security concern if the individual has divided loyalties or foreign financial interests, or is vulnerable to pressure or coercion by a foreign person, group, organization, or government in a manner inconsistent with United States interests.
- **Guideline C: Foreign Preference.** An individual's actions should not indicate a preference for a foreign country over the United States. Individuals who display foreign preference to another country may be prone to provide information or make decisions that are harmful to the interests of the United States. Examples of foreign preference include residence in a foreign country to meet citizenship requirements, possession of a current foreign passport, military service in a foreign country, and receipt of retirement benefits from a foreign country.
- **Guideline D: Sexual Behavior**. An individual's sexual behavior should not leave him or her open to undue influence, exploitation, or duress. Sexual behavior that reflects a lack of judgment or discretion, involves criminal offenses, or indicates a personality or emotional disorder can raise questions about an individual's reliability, trustworthiness and ability to protect classified information. Additionally, sexual relationships with foreign nationals can be a counterintelligence concern.
- **Guideline K: Personal Conduct**. An individual's conduct should not reflect questionable judgment, untrustworthiness, unreliability, lack of candor, dishonesty, or unwillingness to comply with rules and regulations. Failure to cooperate with the security clearance process, including but not limited to failure to meet with a security investigator for a subject interview, omitting, concealing, or falsifying information on security forms, and providing inaccurate and dishonest answers to security officials can constitute a violation of personal conduct.
- **Guideline F: Financial Considerations**. An individual should not place himself or herself at risk for becoming financially overextended. Failure or inability to live within one's means, satisfy debts, and meet financial obligations may indicate poor self-control, lack of judgment, or unwillingness to abide by rules and regulations, all of which can raise concerns about an individual's reliability, trustworthiness and ability to protect classified information. Financial stress can also make individuals more susceptible to outside influence.

- **Guideline G: Alcohol Consumption**. An individual should not excessively consume alcohol to the detriment of judgment, character, or activities, which can lead to the exercise of questionable judgment or failure to control impulses, and can raise questions about an individual's ability to protect classified information.
- **Guideline H: Drug Involvement**: An individual should not be illegally or improperly involved with drugs. Use of illegal drugs or misuse of prescription drugs can raise questions about an individual's ability or willingness to comply with laws, rules, and regulations, as well as his or her social and occupational functioning in the society.
- **Guideline I: Psychological Conditions**. An individual should not suffer from an emotional, mental, or personality condition that causes a significant deficit in his or her psychological, social, and occupational functioning and creates a risk for disclosing classified information. A formal diagnosis of a disorder is not required for there to be a concern under this guideline. Abnormal or bizarre behavior and failure to follow medical advice can both indicate the presence of a psychological condition.
- **Guideline J: Criminal Conduct**. An individual should not have a history or pattern of criminal conduct that casts doubt on his or her judgment, reliability, and trustworthiness. Criminal conduct calls into question a person's ability or willingness to comply with laws, rules and regulations, and may indicate that he or she is likely to commit future criminal behavior. It is important to remember that a clean criminal record does not mean an absence of criminal behavior in the individual's past.
- **Guideline K: Handling Protected Information.** An individual should not, through neglect or premeditation, fail to comply with rules and regulations that protect classified information. Deliberate or negligent failure to protect classified or sensitive information raises doubts about an individual's trustworthiness, judgment, reliability or willingness and ability to safeguard such information, and should be treated as a serious security concern.
- **Guideline L: Outside Activities.** An individual should not be involved with employment or volunteer activities that reflect a conflict of interest with security responsibilities and could create an increased risk of unauthorized disclosure of classified information. Of particular concern are outside activities with the government of a foreign country or a foreign organization.

- **Guideline M: Use of Information Technology Systems.** An individual should not fail to comply with rules and regulations pertaining to Information Technology (IT) systems. Noncompliance may raise security concerns about an individual's reliability and trustworthiness, questioning his or her willingness and ability to properly protect sensitive systems, networks, and information. IT systems include all related computer hardware, software, firmware, and data used for the communication, transmission, processing, manipulation, storage, or protection of information.

All of the Guidelines except for G (Alcohol Consumption) and H (Drug Involvement) were considered in the present research, as it was determined that behaviors in the virtual world cannot involve substance abuse. It should also be noted that at the present moment the Office of the Director of National Intelligence is spearheading an effort to revise the current framework of Adjudicative Guidelines. Interested readers should refer to Kehoe's (2009) report to learn more about the scope and resultant recommendations from this project.

Virtual Environments and Their Place in Culture

Virtual environments are becoming an increasingly popular way for ordinary people to spend their time. They have many uses beyond entertainment, including being a popular tool for business, education, socialization, and even therapy (Mennecke et al., 2008). A key feature of virtual environments is that they function as a persistent universe that continues to exist even when users are offline. Other individuals who are online are able to manipulate surroundings and develop relationships, thereby changing the characteristics of the world while the users are away from their computer. The persistent universe feature provides users with a more immersive experience than the more static online games, stimulating in them feelings of realism and intense engagement (Meadows, 2008). Another feature that users particularly enjoy is the ability to construct their own virtual representation or avatar. Their avatar becomes a vital extension of their real-world persona and can take on many different forms (Castronova, 2007).

There two primary types of virtual environments are online multiplayer games and virtual social environments (Meadows, 2008). Even though many participants in online multiplayer games use them for general social purposes, they have targeted objectives that players must achieve to in order to progress to the next level, such as finding an object or winning a war, and the game developer is the main driver behind creating the rules, objectives, and the appearance of the world. Examples of popular online multiplayer games include World of Warcraft, EVE Online, and Everquest. In contrast, the rules, objectives, and appearance of virtual social environments are largely defined by the users who reside within them. Often, the developer merely provides the platform on which the social environment resides and offers users tools for developing their avatars and physical content. Examples of commonly inhabited virtual social environments include Second Life, Active Worlds, and Kaneva. Second Life was chosen as the setting for the present ethnographic investigation due to its diversity, mass appeal and popularity among users.

Second Life was developed in 2003 by Linden Lab as a virtual 3D social environment, and its users are called residents. After downloading the Second Life viewer and logging on to its software platform or grid, residents can interact with each other using avatars that they create and customize based on their personal preferences. Residents use the Second Life grid to interact, socialize, buy and sell virtual property, participate in groups and activities, and use the platform's creativity tools to build or modify objects and create virtual art. Although some casual observers perceive Second Life to be just a fantasy-filled game, it has a wide range of real-world productivity activities (e.g., virtual meetings, virtual classrooms, product design, etc.), and can be a very real part of some users' daily existence, involving activities that are inextricably intertwined with their real life, even if a user attempts to keep the two separate (Boellstorff, 2008).

Second Life also supports its own virtual economy where the official currency, the Linden Dollar or $L, can be traded for real-life money using the Linden Dollar Exchange. The Linden market, which can be tracked at the LindeXTM Market Data, handles currencies from all over the world including the United States Dollars, Euros, British Pounds, Polish Zlotys, Swedish Kronas, Swiss Francs, Japanese Yens, and others. What is essential to understand is that real-life money is converted to a common currency to generate a world-wide economy that is specific to Second Life and its users (Castronova, 2005; Taylor, 2006). Users can, however, convert Linden Dollars they receive or earn in Second Life to real-world national currencies. For additional background information on Second Life, please refer to the first report in the present series entitled *Cyberculture and Personnel Security: Report I – Orientation, Concerns and Needs* (Leggitt, Shechter, & Lang,

2011). Furthermore, a glossary of common Second Life terms used throughout this report can be found in Appendix A.

Second Life presents three major concerns for personnel security. First, Second Life may allow and enable various adverse or disqualifying behaviors specified in the Adjudicative Guidelines, which at times may be illegal. Second, because these behaviors are occurring in an anonymous and essentially untraceable domain, they will likely not emerge during current background investigations, be detected during automated checks, or be reported through listed or developed references. Third, users' behavior and activities that take place in a virtual world may ultimately affect their job performance, physical and mental health, and real-world functioning by spilling over into their thoughts, feelings, and behavior in the brick-and-mortar world. Detriments to these key areas may undermine an individual's judgment, reliability, and trustworthiness and make him or her unfit to handle classified information.

Of course, Second Life involvement may also lead to positive benefits and experiences, which should not be ignored, but are not the primary focus of this report. Second Life offers many exciting opportunities to its users that may not be readily available in real life, including virtual travel to new countries, expansion of their social circle, and exercise of their imagination to the fullest extent possible. Residents can also use Second Life to make positive changes in how they relate to others in the real world by practicing positive social behaviors in-world first before trying them out in the real world. For example, introverted individuals who experience anxiety during social interactions in the real world can practice starting conversations and developing friendships in Second Life. After a while, they may begin feeling less social anxiety about real-world interactions. Finally, Second Life can be a great educational tool for distance learning, museum-style exhibits, training, or simply as an interactive supplement to traditional classroom learning.

Contents of the Report

This report presents the findings from a 5-month extensive ethnographic investigation into (1) the behaviors of potential security concern that occur within Second Life, and (2) the real-life behavioral spillover resulting from one's involvement in Second Life that may affect individuals' job performance, physical and mental health, and real-world functioning. The method overview section provides full details regarding identification and recruitment of study participants and the data collection techniques that were employed to learn about their involvement in Second Life.

The report is organized into four major sections:

1) Section 1: Behaviors of Personnel Security Concern – the first section identifies the breadth of Second Life behaviors that may be of personnel security concern for each of the relevant Adjudicative Guidelines, and then provides a summary framework that organizes the identified behaviors into four descriptive categories. A small number of the included behaviors raised questions about personnel's ability to function adaptively in the workplace and in the real world. Although not viewed as security risks, these behaviors may undermine employees' ability to perform their job, and would be especially maladaptive for individuals who occupy certain sensitive positions with additional requirements (e.g., requiring superior physical health, sustained vigilance, etc).
2) Section 2: Case Studies – the second section presents 10 case studies that focus on real-life effects of participation in Second Life. They are based on real-world interviews with Second Life residents. These case studies illustrate the experiences of regular Second Life users, and contribute to understanding of both the antecedents and the real-life effects of potentially problematic Second Life involvement.
3) Section 3: Personas – the third section provides a typology that classifies Second Life residents into five personas. The persona categories are based on residents' patterns of Second Life use and potential for personnel security concern.
4) Section 4: General Discussion and Recommendations – the fourth and final section provides a summary of all study findings and contains preliminary recommendations for revising the personnel security vetting process based on the results of the present study.

METHOD OVERVIEW

Introduction to Ethnographic Fieldwork

The earliest example of an anthropologist helping DoD fulfill its mission was Ruth Benedict's contribution to the World War II effort. Benedict was a cultural anthropologist who used her ethnographic skills to research both

Japanese and German cultures during the war and provide the United States government with information that allowed military and diplomatic personnel to achieve their goals by increasing their effectiveness within these cultures. In fact, it was Benedict's recommendation to President Franklin D. Roosevelt that allowed the Emperor of Japan to retain his role after the country's surrender, which was later recognized as a key element in supporting United States interests in the region (Barfield, 1997).

One of anthropology's guiding principles is the concept of cultural relativism. This principle states that an individual or group's behaviors and beliefs should be interpreted through the lens of their own culture, and not from a biased viewpoint of an outsider. Behaviors are examined in their own merit and from a perspective untarnished by value judgments, stereotypes, and what we already know about other cultures. A culturally relativistic approach is particularly essential for the study of new or largely unfamiliar cultures, such as Second Life, as this environment involves norms, beliefs, and behaviors that need to be understood in their own right.

The purpose of utilizing ethnographic techniques is to understand the cultural norms, perspectives, characteristics, and patterns of the cultural system in question and to understand these factors from the perspective of a member of the group. Ervin (2000) describes ethnographic fieldwork as an "omnibus strategy," where a variety of information-gathering techniques that are culturally appropriate for the research objective and the culture in question are employed. Observational methods in anthropology occur on a continuum, from passive observation to immersive participation in a culture. A variety of interview strategies are utilized, including lengthy, open-ended interviews with key respondents; informal conversations with representative samples of informants; and more structured, timed group discussions. In addition to the observation and interviews, ethnographic fieldwork can include formal exercises, such as getting respondents' individual feedback regarding representative photographs or quotes or collecting data about their material culture, such as inventorying a respondent's belongings for a particular research objective.

Ethnographic fieldwork is extremely useful in the early phases of the research process, when the objective is to explore a new culture and describe its prominent behaviors. This approach can yield rich data that can complement the data gathered through traditional survey methods. Anthropologists are trained observers of human behavior, and although the samples they work with are not truly random or representative, they typically try to observe and interview a broad cross-section of informants. Importantly, an anthropologist strives to remain as unbiased as possible when making behavioral observations and drawing judgments, and has no inherent motivation to sway the results in a particular direction. Ultimately, survey methods also have an important place in the research cycle, and they are useful at later stages for determining the quantitative prevalence of specific behaviors and cultural patterns (e.g., how many hours a day a user spends in Second Life). In contrast, ethnographic methods are useful in the early phases of the research process, when the objective is to explore a new culture and develop a rich understanding of the behaviors endemic to it.

Research Participants

Study participants were recruited from the general pool of Second Life users, however all efforts were made to ensure that the final sample resembled cleared personnel as closely as possible. This sampling strategy had one primary advantage. Actual clearance holders might potentially be more dishonest about the nature of their specific activities in Second Life despite being told that their information will be kept confidential and anonymous. Individuals from the general population, on the other hand, might be able to talk about compromising behaviors more openly and honestly. A potential disadvantage of this sampling approach, however, is that the study findings should be interpreted with caution, as there is only evidence to say that they primarily apply to potential (versus actual) clearance holders.

To recruit participants, signs advertising the study were placed in popular Second Life locations including art galleries, dance clubs, shopping malls, the researchers' virtual office, and Second Life classified advertisements. By clicking on the signs, interested participants were able to obtain a copy of a screening questionnaire, fill it out and return it to the researchers' virtual representation in Second Life or avatar. Residents could also obtain a copy of the screening questionnaire by sending an instant message to the researchers.

The target objective of the screening questionnaire presented in Appendix B was to determine if potential participants closely resembled the population of clearance holders in respect to seven key criteria. These criteria included:

- Resident had not participated in a Second Life research study in the past six months.
- Resident was 18 years of age or older.

- Resident was a citizen of the United States and held no dual citizenship with any other country.
- Resident was either employed full-time, self-employed, unemployed and looking for work, or a student.
- Resident has held, currently holds, or would consider holding a job that required a background investigation.
- Resident has been spending at least 5 hours a week in Second Life.
- Resident has been active in Second Life for at least 3 months.

In addition to these requirements, efforts were made to recruit a diverse sample of individuals in respect to socioeconomic status, gender, marital status, and preference for spending in-world time alone vs. with other residents. After analyzing the responses to the screening questionnaires, researchers contacted eligible residents and invited them to participate in the study. Of the 166 residents who applied to participate in the study, 71 met the selection criteria. The recruiting process took approximately 2 weeks.

Research Plan

Consistent with an ethnographic approach, this project used multiple fieldwork methods of data collection chosen by contracted research staff with expertise in both ethnographies and data collection in Second Life. Multiple, convergent methods helped ensure that the gathered information was reliable, valid, and objective. All data were collected and analyzed by two contracted researchers, whereas the development of research and interview questions occurred in collaboration with PERSEREC staff. No Personally Identifying Information (PII) was collected from any respondent throughout the course of the study, and all avatar names have been changed to protect their owners' identities. Although deliberately not collected, there were situations when participants unintentionally shared PII with the contracted researchers. To address this issue, the researchers removed any mention of accidentally shared PII from the data files, transcripts, final analyses, and the final report that were delivered to the PERSEREC staff.

The ethnographic data collection methods used in this study included:

Participant Observation: Participant observation took place throughout the entire 4-month fieldwork period of the 5-month long project. Participant observation represents the backbone of the data collection process, as it provides valuable insight into topics for group discussion sessions and questions for one-on-one interviews with respondents. The technique allows researchers to immerse themselves in the culture, clothing, language, location, and behavior of residents from distinct Second Life sub-cultures. The researchers learned about many unexpected behaviors that they could not have known existed without participating in them alongside other Second Life residents.

Observation: Observation is a much more passive data collection method than participant observation. Observation is frequently employed by researchers who wish to learn about a particular behavior but choose not to participate in the behavior themselves. Examples of Second Life behaviors that were only observed included in-world activities that are illegal in real life, development of romantic relationships with Second Life residents, and partaking in simulated sexual activities in-world. The observation method was also used throughout the entire study, and was valuable for discovering many unexpected behaviors.

Figure 1. A Group Discussion in Second Life Begins.

Sponsored Group Discussions: Group discussion sessions (see Figure 1) allowed researchers to see how avatars relate and communicate with each other in Second Life, and how they talk about their real and second lives. In contrast with observational methods, they provide evidence about levels of personal discomfort that become evident when residents are probed for real-life information. Group discussions laid the groundwork for one-on-one interviews by suggesting what language and approach to use in order to elicit reliable information from the respondents. Finally, they also serve as a recruitment method for selecting a group of core respondents for the one-on-one interviews. Six sponsored group discussions occurred early in the data collection process, each one consisting of three to six residents who met the selection criteria of the screening questionnaire. A total of 28 residents participated in the group discussions.

All group discussions took place in a private skybox in Second Life to protect the anonymity of participants. A skybox is a virtual room placed far away from other users and above the virtual "ground," so that communication and other activities cannot be observed by other residents. A field guide was used to direct the flow of questions asked during the group discussions (see Appendix C). This field guide consisted of open-ended questions organized around the topical areas of Adjudicative Guidelines (e.g., cultural identity, financial influences, psychological conditions, etc.). Although the claims and information provided during group discussions were not verified, researchers took extra care to substantiate and double check the information provided by residents who were recruited for subsequent interviews. This was accomplished through informal conversations during which information was double-checked and cross-referenced, and conversations with residents' in-world friends.

Full disclosure of project goals and informed consent were obtained from all participants prior to the start of the group discussions, and participants were free to leave at any time. The groups followed the text-chat mode of communication because most Second Life users prefer this method, and all discussion logs were transferred to a Microsoft Word document immediately after each discussion was completed. Participants were fully aware that the text-chat was being recorded for subsequent analyses. Finally, all sponsored group discussions participants were compensated for their time in Linden dollars (L$), which were deposited into their Second Life account. Each participant was paid an equivalent of $50 U.S.

Second Life Group Discussions: Researchers also attended 10 Second Life group discussions that varied in the number of participants. These interactive sessions, sponsored by Linden Lab, give residents an opportunity to discuss topics of mutual interest, and they attract a diverse range of avatars. Researchers intentionally attended discussions focused on real-life-Second Life overlap, which allowed them to understand how spillover was affecting residents' daily lives and what type of information residents chose to freely share or not share about this topic. Finally, the Second Life group discussions were an additional way for researchers to recruit potential participants for the one-on-one interviews.

One-on-One Interviews: The purpose of the one-on-one interviews was to explore specific issues brought up by residents during sponsored group discussions, as well as to ask additional questions that were not addressed earlier. In contrast to the group discussions, the interviews were conducted in private in order to create a climate conducive to sharing personal information and telling life stories. Life stories serve as an important ethnographic artifact that sheds light on the impact of Second Life involvement on various facets of real life. Participants were assured that all information they provided would remain anonymous and confidential. Two types of one-on-one interviews were conducted:

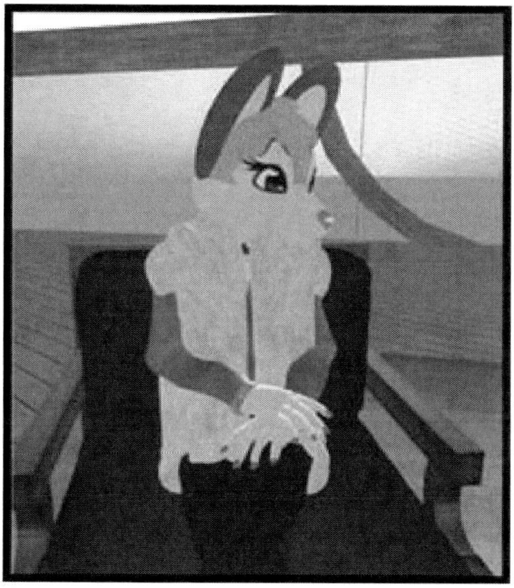

Figure 2. Voice Interview with "Gray".

- **Voice Interviews**: A total of 30 individuals participated in voice interviews via Second Life's voice-chat feature, telephone, or Skype (See Figure 2). These individuals were either recruited through group discussions or contacted based on recommendations of their in-world friends. When asked for permission to record the interviews for later transcription and analysis, all but three respondents consented. Participants were paid in Linden Dollars the equivalent of $75 U.S. for their time, and the payment was deposited directly into their Second Life account.
  The interviews were semistructured and relied on the same field guide that directed the flow of sponsored group discussions (see Appendix C). Participants responded to a series of open-ended questions about various topical areas of the Adjudicative Guidelines. Each voice interview lasted 1.5 to 2 hours.
- **Real-world Interviews**: A subset of individuals who participated in the sponsored group discussions or voice interviews were also interviewed face-to-face. The real-world format of the interviews, though not typical of traditional ethnographies which occur in the subjects' native environment, aka Second Life, was deemed necessary for verifying salient information gathered with the other methods in-world. A total of 10 respondents participated in these interviews. They were selected based on several factors: (1) their willingness to openly and honestly talk about their Second Life involvement and its influence on their real life, (2) a researcher's preliminary assessment of whether their story would provide insight into the major research questions under investigation, and (3) their demographic characteristics. It was the researchers' intent to select a broad sample in respect to gender, age, occupation, socioeconomic status, and United States geographical region. Respondents were interviewed in public locations not requiring the collection of personally identifiable information, such as a coffee shop, in their town of residence.
  A separate field guide provided in Appendix D was developed for the real-world interviews. The researchers had already learned about the respondents' patterns of activity in Second Life from the voice interviews, so their primary goal was to understand how these patterns developed and whether they spilled over into real life. To serve this objective, the interview field guide was organized around various domains of personal functioning (e.g., early childhood, daily activities, work life, family life, health issues, etc.). The interviews

lasted approximately 2 hours and respondents were paid in Linden dollars the equivalent of $300 U.S., The payment was deposited directly into their Second Life account.

SECTION 1: BEHAVIORS OF PERSONNEL SECURITY CONCERN

Method

Four ethnographic data collection methods (participant observation, observation, group discussions, and one-on-one interviews) were used to identify behaviors of personnel security concern within Second Life. The collected data included handwritten field notes from informal conversations with residents, text chat logs from sponsored and Second Life group discussions, and transcripts from recorded voice and face-to-face interviews. This section describes the methods and specific research activities used to identify behaviors of potential security concern. All avatar names have been changed to protect their owners' privacy.

Participant Observation

Participant observation is the act of learning about behaviors by directly engaging in activities. Using this method, two researchers:

- Spent 4 months immersed in Second Life for up to 10 hours a day. Participated in activities such as shopping, building, renting and decorating a home, exploring the various cultures of Second Life, and interacting with other residents.
- Interacted with residents in a variety of settings including strip clubs, role-play areas, shopping malls and villages, coffee houses, bars, dance and live music venues, informal and formal discussions, environmental displays, academic settings, and their Second Life homes.
- Employed two alternative avatar forms in order to gain entry into two popular Second Life sub-cultures that segregate themselves in-world and follow different cultural norms:
    - Gained entry into the anthropomorphic community of Second Life by temporarily becoming a Boston terrier. In Second Life,

this community consists of residents, known colloquially as "furries," who possess both animal and human characteristics. This experience allowed researchers to learn about the norms of this community, as well as the unique cultural characteristics of furry residents who follow these norms.
    - Became a temporary, nonsexual slave-in-training to a Bondage, Discipline, Sadism, & Masochism (BDSM) Master. The BDSM culture is based upon a consensual, sexual tension that is derived from two intentionally unequal sexual roles: the dominant role (also called tops, dominants, or dominatrix) and the submissive role (also called bottoms or subs). In Second Life, participants of the BDSM community construct and propagate an elaborate BDSM culture through strictly enforced roles and virtual photographic techniques (Bardzell, 2006). This experience was particularly useful for understanding how virtual social influence can transfer into real life.
- Spent 4 months developing close relationships with key respondents by associating with them in-world, learning about their real lives, jobs and significant others, observing them react to their Second Life partnerships, and learning about the effects of Second Life on their real-life marriages and other life domains.

Observation

Passive observation was used to gather information about behaviors and activities in which the researchers chose not to participate. Some of the passive observational techniques included:

- Monitoring resident conversations through the open text chat function while exploring Second Life, including shops, dance and music venues, and other public in-world locations.
- Eavesdropping on the open voice chat among residents while exploring Second Life.
- Investigating web-based Second Life blogs and forums, both private and public.
- Taking notes on the public profiles of other residents.
- Using the Second Life search feature to identify groups (e.g., addiction support groups) and locations (e.g., foreign embassies) that could shed light on behaviors of potential personnel security concern.

Group Discussions and One-on-One Interviews

Group discussions and one-on-one interviews gave researchers an opportunity to ask follow-up questions about specific behaviors identified through observation, and to learn about new behaviors that respondents mentioned in response to general questions.

Results

Analysis

The following steps were undertaken to identify behaviors of potential security concern.

- All field notes and text transcripts were uploaded into ATLAS.ti 6, which is a qualitative data analytic tool for synthesizing large bodies of textual, graphical, audio and video information.
- The field notes and transcripts were then coded into distinct behavioral categories. The initial categories were generated using the Adjudicative Guidelines as a topical guide, and as respondents revealed new behaviors of potential concern, additional categories were added to the existing scheme. All reported behaviors were cross-referenced against other available data sources (e.g., other residents) to ensure their veracity.
- An iterative review of the data resulted in the expansion and evolution of the behavioral categories. No reported or observed behaviors were eliminated at any point during the data analysis process (see list of categories and their explanations in Appendix E).

Upon completion of the comprehensive list of observed Second Life behaviors, researchers identified a security-relevant subset of behaviors that raised questions about residents' loyalty, reliability, and trustworthiness. These behaviors are described in detail below for each topical area of the Adjudicative Guidelines A-F and I-M. An additional "lifestyle factors" category was created for behaviors raising broader questions about users' fitness and safety which did not fit under the Adjudicative Guidelines.

Note, that for some of the guidelines, researchers did not obtain direct evidence (i.e., first-hand verbal accounts or personal observations) of occurrence of concerning behaviors, so they included theoretical discussions of what is possible instead. This outcome is not surprising, because these specific disqualifying behaviors (e.g., espionage) also have similarly low base rates in the real-world (Herbig, 2008).

The sections below summarize the findings for each of the Adjudicative Guidelines. Also, some sections are much longer and more detailed than others, which coincides with the observed prevalence and diversity of specific behaviors in Second Life. Subsequently, the length of discussion need not match the potential seriousness of a particular security concern. For example, while *Guideline A: Allegiance to the United States* is given little space compared to *Guideline D: Sexual Behavior*, it simply means that evidence related to sexual behavior is much more common and varied in Second Life. Behaviors related to Allegiance to the United States, while not as common as sexual behaviors, are likely to have a much more direct impact on national security when they do occur. Direct quotes from respondents are inserted whenever possible to illustrate the potential security and safety concerns associated with participation in Second Life.

Also, evidence of concerning behavior was not found for all of the Adjudicative Guidelines.

Guideline A: Allegiance to the United States

Although Second Life can compromise a resident's feelings of national allegiance, it does not allow for physical expression of force or violence in seeking to overthrow, influence, or harm the United States government. Second Life participation, by facilitating socializing across the world, is likely however to increase contact and communication with foreign nationals. No evidence indicating espionage was obtained during the present study, but several hypothetical scenarios are possible. Clearance-holding Second Life residents might compromise classified or sensitive information by unintentionally or intentionally sharing it with foreign agents who are targeting them. On one hand, foreign agents could use social engineering tactics to elicit information or threaten to reveal incriminating details about potentially embarrassing Second Life involvement to friends, coworkers, and significant others. Conversely, cleared insiders seeking to sell information could use Second Life to gain access to foreign individuals, organizations, and virtual embassies. Lack of foreign language knowledge is not a barrier in Second Life, because free language translation tools, available in virtually any language (e.g., Urdu, Farsi, Russian, etc.), make communication with foreigners accessible to all users.

Contact with extremist organizations promoting violence and hostility can, however, be a prevalent behavior in Second Life:

- Residents reported knowing of individuals who participate in gang activities in-world, and also engaging in Second Life gang activity themselves in the past.
- Residents reported knowing of extremist organizations who commit hate crimes directed against select ethnic groups. Several residents even reported being former members of hate groups themselves.

Guideline B: Foreign Influence

The very nature of virtual worlds, where real-world boundaries and borders are nonexistent, allows users to easily associate with anyone from around the world. This affects how the notion of foreign influence should be understood, for there is no need to physically travel to meet and develop relationships with foreign nationals. Second Life allows anonymous participation and self-presentation as one wishes to be seen. Each user controls what information is revealed in his or her public profile or communicated directly.

> "We've never met, but (my master) knows my first name. I know his first name. He has my phone number just because he texts me. I have his, obviously. But he lives in another country, which is fine."
>
> ~ "Beth," suburban mom

It is trivially easy in Second Life to contact people who self-identify as being from European, Asian, and Middle Eastern countries, and conversely, it is equally impossible to know the true identities of purported United States citizens. Barring external identity proofing measures, users can never know whether they are communicating with a member of Taliban versus a retired nurse in Seattle. This ambiguity opens the door to foreign agents and other hostile parties who wish to assess and recruit individuals with access to sensitive and/or classified information. They may do so by using social engineering tactics to build trust with the individual and by claiming to be from the same culture. In such a scenario, a user could become less cautious about the kinds of information they reveal.

In sum, residents' personal accounts of Second Life experiences led to the following observations:

- The perceived anonymity of Second Life can create a false sense of security and make residents more susceptible to foreign influence from others. Individuals who entered Second Life as a way to escape real-life problems may be especially vulnerable to influence by those who wish to manipulate them. The anonymity creates a false sense of protection, where residents feel safer revealing vulnerable thoughts and feelings than they would in person, or if their real-life identity and visage were exposed.
- Enhanced emotional vulnerability can make Second Life residents who are looking for acceptance, understanding, and love more susceptible to influence. "Newbies," which is a derogatory term used to identify new residents in Second Life, arc also more easily lead into compromising virtual sexual activities or extramarital relationships that occur within Second Life. This influence, while consensual, is a security risk because it opens up avenues for coercion and pressure by foreign citizens, groups, and organizations.
- Some residents intentionally avoid contact with individuals from foreign countries. It is salient for these residents to be able to communicate with others with ease, and it is important to them that their interlocutors have an excellent command of English language, and understand the associated abstract references and slang. This group of residents tends to be somewhat ethnocentric and seeks out only those who come from similar cultural backgrounds.
- Residents who engage with foreigners typically do so because of a preexisting interest in cultures and languages that stems from real life. In fact, some of these individuals also report having foreign pen pals in real life found through such Internet websites as Penpal International, and some even report having foreign spouses. Specifically:
    - Some residents develop relationships with individuals who reside in United States-allied countries (e.g., Canada, France, etc.), but claim that those relationships do not affect their loyalty to the United States. They report perceiving a sense of common values from these interactions and engaging in such in-world activities as watching music performances, talking about movies, checking out art exhibits, etc.

- Some residents befriend individuals from underprivileged countries and feel that their loyalty to the United States has increased as a result of these friendships. After learning about how difficult life can be in certain corners of the world, many individuals reported feeling more appreciative of their lives in the United States. In sum, finding out about challenges in housing, medical care, finances, and lack of individual rights educates previously uninformed residents about the benefits of being an American citizen.
- Some residents interact with foreigners from countries hostile to the United States, but they find themselves more strongly allied to the United States after these interactions. This occurs because individuals from hostile countries sometimes attack residents from the United States verbally, making them feel as though they were provoked without due cause. Residents report that they approached hostile foreigners with good intentions or by accident, and feel as though they did not deserve the attack they received. In the end, they decided to remove themselves from such situations because they did not want to experience any more hostility.

Guideline C: Foreign Preference

Although Second Life does not provide a platform for direct exercise of foreign preference (e.g., possessing a foreign passport, voting in a foreign election, etc.), it provides easy access to foreign individuals, organizations, and embassies who can influence residents to commit these acts. Residents can also engage in various behaviors that may enhance their preference for other countries. Examples of these behaviors include:

- Residents sometimes create an avatar in the form of a citizen from an admired country and then behave accordingly to this country's cultural customs and norms.
- Some residents unintentionally or intentionally interact with residents from a specific country, and then become highly interested in this country after learning more about it. This can include an interest in the country's language or food choices, marriage and child-rearing customs, music, politics, etc. Second Life provides opportunities for

practicing foreign languages, marrying foreign citizens in-world, finding foreign citizens in Second Life who agree to meet in real life, visiting foreign embassies of various countries that exist in Second Life, etc.

- Some residents seek out cultures of choice that they had an affinity for before getting involved in Second Life, and may enter the virtual world for the sole purpose of increasing their exposure to that culture. Second Life allows them to meet more people from the countries of interest and develop friendships or romantic relationships with them. This can provide additional opportunities for real-life meetings and visits to foreign countries.
- Some residents' interactions with other cultures have been so negative that their preference for a specific culture actually diminished. Specifically, several respondents reported being turned off to Italy after receiving overt sexual advances from users claiming to be Italian men.

Guideline D: Sexual Behavior

The anonymous nature of Second Life sets a comfortable stage for experimenting with risky sexual behaviors that many individuals would not pursue in real life. To the extent that a user feels the need to hide such fantasy behaviors from family, friends, or colleagues, virtual sex may be a potential security risk through use of blackmail. While virtual sex without physical contact is generally legal in the United States, as is viewing pornography and participating in video or phone sex, Second Life provides another domain of potential concern. Virtual sexual behaviors and extramarital relationships might alter residents' real-life value systems and affect their real-world relationships with romantic partners. As sexual behavior is extremely common and diverse in Second Life, the discussions provided copious evidence for many potentially risky behaviors. The details are described below:

Virtual Sex Work

Second Life sex workers or escorts can be found in many dance clubs, escort hubs, and other locales. Each escort sets his or her boundaries about the activities that will be permitted, to almost always include in-world fantasy sex using text chat, but sometimes also video sex, voice/phone sex, or even real-world contact. People who would never consider working in the sex industry in real life are reported to be more willing to participate in simulated sex in Second Life. Some can be the proverbial soccer mom in the real world, yet become an escort to earn extra money. Escorts are extremely easy to find in Second Life, and work from their real-life locations. Conversely, foreign agents could also pose as escorts, in an attempt to manipulate Second Life users whom they wish to target and/or assess.

> "I can say that I have had special clients that I still entertained in-world that are kind of, I don't want to say high rollers, but I guess their status is higher."
>
> ~ "Shannon," suburban mom.

One example of a Second Life escort is respondent "Shannon." She is a married mother of a two-year-old daughter who works part-time in real life. Her husband works and goes to school full-time, so he is rarely at home. Shannon has worked as a stripper and an escort in Second Life and, and although she no longer seeks new clients, she continues to provide regular services to at least two people. One is in Italy, and the other is in Saudi Arabia. She admits to interacting with them using both voice calls and webcam. Shannon's behavior illustrates the ease through which Second Life users can enter relationships with individuals claiming to be foreigners.

> "My wife had breast cancer and Second Life was a way for me to keep my sanity without feeling like I was leaving her alone in the house."
>
> ~ "Larry"

Virtual Extramarital Sex

Virtual extramarital sex is widespread in Second Life. Some residents are involved in Second Life simply because they can participate in a wide range of sexual experiences unavailable through a real-life partner. As with virtual sex work, the emphasis on fantasy and the lack of physical contact changes how many people view such behaviors. Residents view cyber sexual relations as being less morally compromising than real-life sex, because they lack physical contact. Furthermore, they feel that virtual sex is logistically easier to coordinate than trying to meet someone in real life, and can even be conducted at the keyboard while a real-life spouse is present nearby.

Second Life virtual sex takes on three main forms:

- Sex is simulated in graphical, animated detail, akin to a modern 3D computer or video game, between two or multiple avatars and observed by the corresponding avatar owners on each computer. The participants narrate what is going on, what each person is feeling, and what each person is doing, in a way that extends beyond the capabilities of the on-screen animation. Written text is universally available, and the integrated voice chat enables residents to communicate in real time.
- Sex occurs with written or verbal communication only, where the two avatars may remain fully clothed on the computer screen and appear to other avatars as just sitting or dancing.
- Interest in sexual activity is expressed in Second Life, but both parties agree to take the interaction to an outside webcam environment. In these instances Second Life serves as merely a meeting ground.

Some residents state that they participate in Second Life virtual sex merely to meet a biological sexual need. They see no overlap between their virtual sexual activities and their relationships with real-life partners, and consider the two domains to be separate categories because Second Life provides little emotional involvement and the activities are not real. Others become emotionally invested in Second Life relationships and view them as similar to their real-world relationships. Some residents even report that their Second Life sexual encounters are more intense than their real-life encounters because of the imagination and attentiveness required on both parts to achieve what they see as a satisfying experience. In their words, "Someone can't just lay there and do nothing, like in real life."

As with real-life, sexual involvement with Second Life partners can either be pursued deliberately or it can happen unintentionally. Intentional virtual sex involves purposefully seeking out sexual companionship in-world, while unintentional relationships develop as a byproduct of other activities and social experiences. Residents who report unintentional sexual encounters are more prone to feelings of guilt about their actions than those who actively pursue cyber sex. Both types of Second Life users may be at risk for discovery or blackmail if they are hiding their behavior from spouses, friends, and co-workers.

Residents report several reasons for why they engage in virtual extramarital sex:

- Boredom in their real-life marriage and a strong desire for excitement.
- Pursuit of an emotional and physical connection that is lacking in their real-life relationship.
- Distraction during times of temporary stress or conflict in their marriage.
- Relief and companionship during times when a spouse is ill, such as from cancer treatments.

Compromising Sexual Experimentation

Many Second Life residents report that they role play or experiment with issues arising from sexuality (e.g., rape), homosexuality or bisexuality, and sexual fetishes (e.g., BDSM). While these behaviors do not constitute a security risk when conducted in a private, consensual, and discreet manner, the perceived anonymity and accelerated nature of Second Life relationships may provide a false sense of security and, therefore, increase the chances of malicious, intentional discovery and real-life exposure of such activities. As discussed in Report I, anonymity can lead to online disinhibition or greater comfort in revealing real-life information or sharing personal details, and software security is always imperfect and breakable. Subsequently, those participants who feel their anonymity in Second Life is absolute and guaranteed, and who feel their experimental activities must be hidden from friends, family, and associates, may have a limited understanding of the security risks of participation.

Age-Play

According to Second Life's developer Linden Lab, age-play entails "real-life images, avatar portrayals, and other depictions of sexual or lewd acts involving or appearing to involve children or minors." (Linden Lab, 2007). This definition includes avatars that are child-sized, have child-like features, wear child-like clothing, or communicate using child-like verbiage or actions. Although age-play has been officially banned by Linden Lab, it is still present in a form that skirts the boundaries or violates the policy.[1] Child avatar bodies and clothing can still be purchased in numerous locations across Second Life. Child avatars were also observed in public places with coquettish stances and using language that was child-like and teasing. Not only is age-play against Linden Lab's Terms of Service Agreement (TSA; Linden Lab, 2010a), but it also may be illegal in a virtual cyber context because of its close associations with child pornography. Moreover, it is a potential security risk to the extent that is symptomatic of an underlying mental health condition that may affect the individual's judgment, reliability, and trustworthiness.

Bestiality

Simulated sexual contact with animals or bestiality is another behavior of potential security concern that occurs in Second Life. Residents who engage in this behavior sometimes take steps to protect the locations where its members meet to engage in zoophytical acts. Interested individuals must either privately contact the owners of zoophile groups to gain access to special playgrounds that exist for taking part in or observing virtual sex with animals or they can find some of them through Second Life's search feature. Bestiality can become a security risk if it reflects an underlying psychological condition that undermines the resident's judgment and reliability or of it leads to vulnerabilities such as blackmail.

From a potential blackmail standpoint, it may be important to differentiate the bestiality culture from the furry culture. While bestiality followers simulate or participate in sexual acts with animals, furries are humans wearing animal costumes. Furries in Second Life choose this form for a variety of reasons, only some of which are attributed to sexual desire.

Guideline E: Personal Conduct

Second Life has a large fantasy component for many users, and if real-world standards are applied to its culture, violations of the personal conduct guideline occur routinely. Different users approach Second Life with different expectations. Some see it as a place for role-playing and games, others seek to conduct real-life business, and some apparently perceive it to be an alternative dating site. Many lie, misrepresent themselves, or exercise questionable judgment in social interactions or relationships with other Second Life residents. Although these behaviors may raise questions about trustworthiness, it is unclear whether those engaged in fantasy activities would also fail to cooperate with the demands of the security clearance process or fail to comply with security-relevant rules and regulations. The following behaviors, potentially indicative of personal conduct violations, surfaced during the discussions:

Lying

Lying takes several forms in Second Life, but must be clearly differentiated from role-play behavior. Upon first joining Second Life, a user must choose one of a handful of default male or female avatars to represent themselves in-world. Immediately after joining, one can purchase or freely obtain a wide range of alternative bodies, clothing, and accessories to create a character fitting a specific role. The chosen role may be highly similar to the user's real-life identity or it may be completely different, to include the opposite gender, robots, animals, and more. Those who focus on role play immerse themselves in a character as an actor does on stage or film. Many users also explain the role-play function of a character in a public profile (e.g., preference for companionship with a certain sex, the desire to play a dominant or submissive role, interest in vampire fiction or science fiction, etc.).

Fantasy role play meant to provide a rich depiction of a character must be distinguished from lying with a deliberate intention to deceive others. Lying in Second Life occurs when residents deliberately provide others with false information about themselves or their real lives while presenting this information as being true. Lying is different than role-play in that liars deceive for their own gain, and allow others to believe that this information is true. The anonymous nature of the environment of lack of means to verify claims increases the potential for forms of deception that would be impossible in the real world. Perhaps the most ubiquitous example is that men in real life create highly attractive female avatars and then seek cyber sex or relationships with either male or female avatars. This practice is so common that many users present their views on real-life gender in their public profiles. According to respondents, when real gender is systematically concealed through lies, it has been noted to have particularly negative effects on real-life lesbians in Second Life who seek real female companions.

Residents in Second Life lie for two main reasons:

- Protection: Some residents wish to remain completely anonymous in Second Life and go to great lengths to protect their real identity. As a result, they lie about many of their real-life characteristics, such as gender, place of residence, occupation, marital status, and other identifying information. A potential security risk is present if these activities are hidden from family, friends, and coworkers. Despite great efforts to conceal who they are in real life, they are not immune to discovery and exposure by a malignant actor who figures out their real-life identity.

- Personal Gain: Some residents lie to obtain tangible services or information from those around them. For example, men will pretend to be women to gain access to virtual sexual experiences with real-life lesbians, or people will lie about their health status to gain sympathy or entertainment from telling their story to others. Individuals will also lie about their real-life marital status to make themselves more appealing to potential partners.

Hacking, Manipulation, and Extortion

Hacking, manipulation, and extortion activities that occur in Second Life are meant to intimidate and/or influence other residents. Individuals who instigate these behaviors exhibit a lack of judgment and trustworthiness and their behavior raises concerns about their ability to safeguard classified information. Examples of these behaviors include:

- Griefing or harassing other Second Life residents. The objective of griefing is to cause annoyance to others for the purpose of personal enjoyment. Examples of griefing include using third-party hacking programs, insulting and intimidating other residents, trying to steal property belonging to others, etc.
- Becoming a part of a Second Life intimidation gang that may even transcend the virtual boundaries and extend into the real world.
- Recruiting unsuspecting new members to become a part of communities that practice alternative lifestyles (e.g., BDSM role-play) by using various deception techniques.
- Using scripts to gain access to IP addresses and, through IP address geolocation, real-life locations down to the city or general region.
- Blackmailing other residents for personal gain by threatening to expose their Second Life activities.

Guideline F: Financial Considerations

Second Life can be used for business, hobbies, or social activities, and as with other areas of life, people can sometimes experience money-related or financial problems. Residents reported several behaviors of potential security concern that bear on the ability to control personal spending and satisfy financial obligations. The Linden dollar ($L) can be purchased using a credit card or a PayPal account, and then converted into a variety of international currencies using the Linden Dollar Exchange. Although Linden Lab outlawed official gambling in 2007, residents report that it still exists and is easily accessible to those who seek it out. Discussions with residents identified the following behaviors of potential security concern:

Overspending

Some residents report heavy spending on Second Life goods and services, with totals ranging between $150-2500 (U.S.) a month. The implications of overspending on virtual goods and services are mixed. Some individuals report that it has caused them real-life financial hardships, while others say that their Second Life expenses are completely justified because they take the place of other entertainment expenditures (e.g., going to the movies or meeting up for lunch with real-life friends). If overspending in Second Life materially contributes to real-life financial hardship or credit problems, then such behavior indicates a clear lack of responsibility and participation may be especially risky for individuals who are already financially overstretched.

> "I've spent so much more of my money in this damn thing than I ever thought I was going to when I first started up.'
>
> ~ "Laura'

Scams

Residents report being duped out of their money when individuals tell them of real-life financial hardships that are not actually true. Stories of unpaid bills, disabilities preventing real-life income, or abusive spouses who do not work have been reported, and can be accompanied by requests for help. Although helping an individual in need is admirable in some situations, giving a significant amount of money to someone in cyberspace without any ability to verify his or her story may indicate a lack of judgment.

Blackmail

Some individuals reported being subject to blackmail when another resident, who was aware of their real-life identity, threatened to expose their activities if they did not provide them with some form of compensation. In one specific instance, a neighbor, who had originally introduced a resident to Second Life, threatened to expose her unless she gave up her sim or piece of Second Life land. The resident ended up complying and giving up her sim, worth approximately $250 (U.S.). Depending on the perceived costs associated with exposure and discovery, residents might go to great lengths to satisfy the blackmailer's demands.

Guideline I: Psychological Conditions

A serious concern for personnel security is that some individuals may become clinically addicted to Second Life. Cyber addiction or compulsive cyber use is behaviorally similar to other forms of addiction (e.g., alcohol, drugs, etc.), and it may severely impair an employee's judgment, reliability, and trustworthiness. Unfortunately, there is very little awareness among both clinicians and laypeople about the symptoms and consequences of compulsive cyber use, so this disorder can often go untreated. In addition to addiction, residents also reported experiencing a great amount of cognitive interference from Second Life to real life, feelings of paranoia, feelings of reduced guard, and an increased desire to control all aspects of one's environment in real life.

Compulsive Cyber Use

Second Life contains many addictive features that may induce some users to spend lengthy periods of time in-world. It offers residents a more enjoyable escape from real-life problems than television, by allowing them to write the script that controls their life, rather than passively watch other actors read parts of the script written by someone else. They talk of time speeding by in Second Life, where they intend to sit down for 20 minutes to complete a simple task, only to realize later that 3 hours have passed.

> "And Second Life was almost like my new booze. I would log on without any reason to log on. The visual stimulation alone was sort of addicting, and then the illusion of being surrounded by friends, you know, which generally are people who don't really know you and you're able to put your best foot forward."
>
> ~ "Luisa"

Because of its addictive potential, Second Life might be particularly maladaptive for individuals with existing clinical addictions (e.g., alcohol, drugs). Residents who have gone through rehab reported that they feel as though Second Life takes the place of alcohol or drugs, allowing them to forget about their real-life problems and, therefore, not address them. Instead of being chemically altered they become digitally altered.

Many residents reported that Second Life has become an addiction that they don't want to live without, sometimes coming at the expense of real-life marriages, jobs, and friends. Of the 166 Second Life residents who applied to be a part of the study, 104 (62.7%) reported being in Second Life for at least 20 hours a week or more. For the subset of individuals selected for voice and real-world interviews, it was not unusual to be in-world for closer to 30 or 40 hours a week. Interestingly, some of the heavy users who participated in one-on-one interviews were much more candid about the amount of time they spend in Second Life during the voice interviews than during the real-world interviews. For example, individuals who reported spending 6 or 7 hours a day in Second Life changed those numbers to 1 or 2 hours a day during real-world interviews.

Cognitive Interference or "Split World" Effect

Residents also reported experiencing cognitive interference from Second Life to real life that would occur after spending many hours in-world at a time. Images of Second Life and real life would begin to blur together, and they would feel as though they were experiencing their real life through a Second Life lens. They would begin looking in their real-life closets for clothing they only own in Second Life, or would experience sudden urges to edit a piece of real furniture by moving it or changing its fabric. Some even reported beginning to emulate their Second Life avatar's posture and appearance in real life. The presence of cognitive interference is a potential security concern, because it suggests that heavy Second Life users may start confusing the rules of conduct in the brick-and-mortar world with the rules of conduct in Second Life.

Paranoia and Reduced Guard

Second Life allows for anonymous participation, which on one hand opens the door to exploration and experimentation, but on the other hand creates doubts about the identities of in-world contacts. Some people frequently use alternate avatars or alts, and can therefore purposefully befriend the same person under multiple guises. This can lead to excessive worry that others are being deceitful in both Second Life and real life. Some users even reported feeling that their romantic partners or friends in real life are purposefully deceiving them or cheating on them.

"It felt sneaky, like if someone comes to your door and you don't answer, you hide. And I felt like he was hiding that way from me. So that drama really hurt my feelings."

~ "Joanne"

In contrast, other residents have reported that they have become almost too trusting, and have lost the natural wariness that typically prevents the disclosure of personal information to strangers. The potential cause of this uninhibited disclosure may be explained by Second Life's emphasis on anonymity, fun activities, and a bias toward socialization, which promotes opening up to others more quickly than in real life. For personnel security interests, the important question is whether extensive participation in such a culture might lead individuals to become too trusting and inadvertently reveal sensitive facts about themselves or their job to other Second Life residents.

Control

Second Life allows users to design, control, and manipulate most aspects of their in-world lifestyle and environment, in this manner providing a heightened level of control that is absent in real life. For many residents this is one of Second Life's most attractive features. Individuals can control not only their personal appearance and the appearance of their surroundings, but also their level and content of communication with other residents. The ability to remain anonymous gives them a level of control over what others can find out about them, and gives them the option to walk away from an avatar and create a new one, without notice to friends they have in Second Life. Of course, the perceived sense of control and anonymity is not absolute, because interested individuals can figure out someone's real-life identity through various hacking mechanisms, and Linden Lab and law enforcement agencies have legal grounds for accessing personal details in certain contexts.

Guideline J: Criminal Conduct

Criminal conduct is a core personnel security concern because it raises questions about individuals' ability to make sound decisions and follow laws. Second Life crime largely resembles that of the real world and other online environments. The greatest potential difference is that what occurs in Second Life is unlikely to appear on criminal records or surface during a background investigation. Per observation, paid virtual sex work may be the most prevalent criminal activity in-world, but there is no known data on how frequently virtual sex work that occurs in Second Life results in illegal real-world sex work. Sex work was addressed under Guideline D: Sexual Behavior, and other criminal behaviors reported by residents are described below. All of the behaviors below are crimes in both real life and Second Life.

Illegal Computer Activities

As with all commercial computer environments, certain activities such as hacking the system to identify IP addresses, hacking into accounts, and using scripted CopyBots or debugging tools to steal other residents' copyrighted content, is illegal in Second Life. Yet residents with technical knowledge and experience say that such activities are not that difficult to accomplish despite the given constraints. Linden Lab admits that there is at least one way that IP addresses can be accessed in Second Life and recommends a fix to this problem, but the burden of protection lies with each resident (Linden Lab, 2010b). Residents without the ability to implement the security solution are subject to an elevated risk of having their real-life identities discovered by cyber intruders.

In addition, the Second Life Viewer 2.0 software released in 2010 includes a media sharing option which allows cyber intruders even more access to individuals' private IP addresses. This access leaves many Second Life residents concerned about their privacy. IP-Geolocation allows others, with only an IP address, to pinpoint an individual's physical location at the time he or she is using the computer. One company providing such services is MaxMind. According to MaxMind's website, their IP-Geolocation technology (MaxMind, 2008) provides businesses with a noninvasive way to determine geographical and other information about their Internet visitors in real-time. When a person visits their website, geolocation technology can determine the visitor's country, region, city, postal code, and area code. Furthermore, this technology can also provide such information as longitude/latitude, connection speed, Internet Service Provider (ISP), company name, domain name, and whether the IP address is an anonymous proxy or a satellite provider. Although MaxMind's technology was designed for industry purposes, individual cyber intruders can take advantage of it just the same to assist in figuring out a resident's real-life identity.

Gang Activities

Concerns about gang activity in Second Life have existed ever since its inception in 2003. Second Life gangs (e.g., Patriotic Nigras, 4Chan, etc.) have been associated with forcing residents out of public areas and behaving as though they own them, bullying and intimidating residents who disagree with them, and stealing Second Life property of other residents (Reuters, 2008). For example, in 2008, a gang called Patriotic Nigras raided the headquarters of John Edwards's presidential election campaign office in Second Life, causing a big media stir (Jenkins, 2010). Gangs who have their roots in Second Life are also bleeding over into real life. These groups and others get shut down by Linden Labs, but residents report that they soon reappear under new names or host sites outside Second Life. The groups generally have websites or chat rooms that members can access for instructions on how to join them. Although only a fraction of residents reported direct personal involvement in gang activities, there were many reports of being direct victims of gang crimes and of hearing that others they know participate in gangs.

> "4Chan has taken over people's My Space, they've taken over people's Second Life. They've taken over so many things if they had the right amount of information. For example, one of my friends kept getting phone calls saying that one of them was going to kill them."
>
> ~ "Kevin"

Hate Crimes

The Linden Lab TSA specifically prohibits hate-crime activity by stating that individuals cannot "post, display or transmit content that is obscene, hateful, or racially, ethnically or otherwise objectionable" (Linden Lab, 2010a). Unfortunately, inflammatory hate-crime language and activities can still be observed in Second Life, and various hate groups (e.g., white supremacists) use it to coordinate activities in-world and, possibly, in real life. Residents reported knowing about a Nazi supremacist hate group called "Furzi," which Linden Lab officially banned in 2007. Although Furzis were not formally related to the furry culture in Second Life, they used furry avatars to openly campaign anti-Semitic messages and built gas chambers within Second Life for role-play purposes. It is not clear if and how residents participate in hate groups among residents, but a search for avatar names revealed a large number of names reflecting anti-Semitic or racist viewpoints.

Several residents also reported direct involvement in Second Life hate groups that occurred in their past.

Drug Trafficking

Several residents reported first-hand knowledge of others using Second Life to promote real-life drug trafficking. Drug dealers meet at public sandboxes, which are areas dedicated to designing and building objects, or on private lands to coordinate buying and selling of drugs in the United States. Most of this activity likely takes place through private instant messaging, but one resident reported hearing an open-voice chat conversation in a public location between two drug dealers. Another respondent, who in real life had been in trouble for criminal activity, knew of friends who would set up real-life drug deals through Second Life. In these instances, however, it is difficult to determine whether observed behaviors involved actual plans to meet in real life or they were part of role-play.

> I was scared that they'd be there in open voice talking about selling and trading (drugs) and other things. If they'd do that what else would they do? So I got out of there."
>
> ~ "Evan"

Guideline K: Handling Protected Information

The perceived anonymity of Second Life, coupled with a heightened sense of closeness to other residents, often results in individuals revealing personal information in-world that they would never share in real life. Although most of the potentially harmful information disclosure likely happens unintentionally, residents seeking to make a profit or satisfy the demands of someone who is threatening to expose their Second Life activities could also be disclosing sensitive information deliberately and knowingly. From a personnel security perspective, the virtual context of Second Life does not lend itself to supervision and monitoring to the same degree as the real-world context, and therefore may be an ideal setting for transmitting sensitive information. Residents report that several factors contribute to their willingness to share personal facts with strangers whose real-life identity is unknown.

> "... the fact that my email address ends in pentagon.mil, talk about being in a regulated, controlled environment. It's just been culture shock for me. It's as extreme as being taken out of my city dwellings and thrown into an aboriginal tribe and saying, 'OK, you're one of them now.'"
>
> ~ "Ken"

Anonymity

The perception of anonymity in Second Life provides residents with a false sense of protection and freedom about sharing personal information in-world. They report thinking that as long as they do not reveal their real name or location, any information they share with others about their personal life or job cannot be traced back to them. However, as discussed earlier, scripts exist that allow nefarious individuals to obtain IP addresses and gain access to real-life identities (Linden Lab, 2010b), making the promise of anonymity in Second Life a false one. In addition, IP-Geolocation allows individuals to immediately identify the country, region, city, zip code, area code, ISP, company name, and other identifying parameters of any IP address that is transmitted from the Second Life server to an active website.

Heightened Sense of Closeness

Residents report that they feel an extreme sense of emotional closeness to other Second Life users, who can be more important to them than their real-world family and friends. These strong bonds and perceptions of trust develop quickly and at times without deliberate intent. For example, residents who joined Second Life for work purposes never intended to also participate in its dynamic social culture. As they spent more time in-world, made friends, and experienced a range of unimaginable activities, Second Life became an integral part of their real lives. Some business users also report starting emotional relationships with other residents—a possibility they never imagined beforehand. The security risk is that some individuals may become too comfortable sharing sensitive information with their Second Life friends, lovers, and associates, when they have no way of determining their motives or their national identity.

Self-Expression

Second Life facilitates and encourages behaviors that many participants would never do in real life. This occurs both during fantasy role-play where the intent is to take on the identity of one's avatar, and also when trying out behaviors that may be too risky or anxiety-provoking in real life. The wariness characteristic of face-to-face interactions with strangers also decreases in Second Life, possibly increasing the chances for confusion about when it is appropriate to discuss private or sensitive information. For example, some residents report using Second Life to act flirtatious in ways that are not socially acceptable in real life, while several others reported using Second Life to practice being more open and conquer real-world shyness. Increased openness resulting from participation raises questions about individuals' ability to discern between when it is appropriate to share personal information and when it is not.

Guideline L: Outside Activities

Second Life in itself is an outside activity that may pose a conflict of interest to an employee's security responsibilities because it allows individuals to take part in groups and visit Second Life locations that are openly and formally associated with foreign embassies, international organizations, and hostile domestic groups. However, due to the often anonymous and fantasy nature of participation, it is not entirely clear whether such actions fall under traditional concerns about outside activities per the Adjudicative Guidelines. Second Life offers numerous opportunities for interacting with or volunteering for foreign groups, and one might not even be able to determine the national origin of these organizations. In addition, some groups claim to promote tourism and business for their home culture, while their true objectives might be different.

Moreover, because subjects are not explicitly asked about their cyber involvement at any point during the background investigation process, their Second Life activities are highly likely to go undetected. Individuals may also use the lack of real-world contact as justification for failing to report their Second Life involvement. Discussions with residents provided direct support for the following outside activities that may be of potential security concern:

- **Foreign Embassies:** Residents can visit foreign embassies and interact with their staff. Examples of Second Life foreign embassies include Sweden's "Second House of Sweden" and Estonia's "Virtual Estonia." Both locations offer cultural information and facilitate social activities, while Estonia's embassy provides a kiosk to apply for a visa.

- **Foreign Groups:** Residents can also belong to various foreign groups and organizations, such as "Najd," an unofficial Saudi Arabian group with over 1,500 members based at a Second Life location called "The Kingdom of Saudi Arabia." Notices provided by the group are in Arabic. Iran also has groups dedicated to it, including "Iranians" with 93 members, designated as being for "true Iranians who love Iran" and "Iran" with 288 members. Iraq also has a group associated with it, but researchers' request to review the group was denied.

Guideline M: Use of Information Technology Systems

Second Life, by virtue of being computer software, inherently presents opportunities for noncompliance with IT access rules. The entire virtual world is created through code and scripts for objects, animations, poses, and movements. Individuals with no real computer programming experience can participate in scripting and coding in-world, thanks to Second Life's online tutorials. Those with programming knowledge can and do manipulate the Second Life technical infrastructure for a variety of purposes, potentially raising concerns about their ability to follow IT rules and procedures. Note that all of these behaviors are illegal in Second Life and are against the Linden Lab TSA. It is of potential concern to personnel security that individuals who misuse IT systems in-world and take advantage of Second Life's open source environment, might also be at an increased risk for abusing IT rules in the workplace.

Griefing

Griefing is a Second Life term for activities that resemble flaming or trolling in other online environments. Griefers seek to irritate, harass, and assault other Second Life residents, generally through subversive coding scripts. The typically engage in disruptive behavior for attention and fame, tend to target public areas, and often focus their efforts on naïve newbies. Examples of Second Life griefing activities include virtual bombs that litter areas with debris, scripts that burn buildings, and scripts that rain sexual objects on attendees during business meetings. Although Linden Lab sometimes suspends accounts of reported griefers, they often reappear under a different avatar name only to continue their disruptive activities.

CopyBots

CopyBots are debugging tools that allow users to export embedded objects that are copyrighted and intended to be sold for profit from Second Life into a computer file, and then use them for personal gain. Using CopyBots in Second Life is the virtual equivalent of stealing from an individual or a store in real life. This behavior angers original owners of the objects, and in particular, business owners who create and sell objects for profit. Although CopyBots undermine emerging property rights of Second Life residents, no centralized or formal effort has been undertaken by Linden Lab to eradicate their use.

Hacking

Computer savvy users can also use hacking techniques to discover other residents' IP addresses and find out their real-life identities (e.g., through IP-Geolocation), take control of their avatars, and steal their in-world currency. Hacking behavior that occurs in-world raises potential security concerns about an individual's ability to properly use IT systems in the workplace.

Other: Lifestyle Factors

A number of frequently observed and reported behaviors did not directly fall under the security considerations outlined in the Adjudicative Guidelines framework, however, they could undermine employees' ability to perform their duties effectively and be productive in the workplace. All of the behaviors in this category relate to the negative impact of excessive Second Life involvement on health, real-world functioning and relationships, and job performance. In some contexts, they might also also raise questions about individuals' judgment, reliability, and trustworthiness.

Neglect of Family and Friends

Second Life is a complex and engaging environment for its users, as it provides many activities and forms of entertainment that can replace many core functions of television, films, books, social clubs, and bars. For those who have trouble managing responsibilities, involvement can exert a heavy toll on users' personal lives. Residents who report spending a lot of time in-world, often end up neglecting their real-life family and friends. At times, they replace a real-life significant other with relationships and friendships formed in Second Life. For example, it is not uncommon for individuals to have

Second Life "partners," "brothers," "sisters" and "mothers," or less commonly even go through the Second Life pregnancy process to have a "baby."

> "I've been in Second Life with chat on and heard people yelling at their kids, telling their two-year-old to go get them a drink because they don't want to get up from the game, and it's sad. It's very sad."
>
> ~ "Catherine"

Some Second Life residents report that their family and friends complain to them about the amount of time they spend in-world. Others adamantly deny neglecting their own children, but readily tell stories of others they know who neglect their children. Many marriages have been broken up over a spouse's excessive preoccupation with Second Life and complete withdrawal from the family. Similarly, many friendships have been put on hold because residents who spend extensive periods of time in-world have little time for real-world social interactions.

Neglect of Personal Health

Extended hours spent in-world may lead to the neglect of proper exercise, diet, and self-care required for a balanced life. Residents report perceiving that time passes more quickly in Second Life than in real life, resulting in missed exercise routines, meals, showers, and sleep. They also report that extended time spent at the computer causes such issues as anxiety attacks, back and neck strain, carpal tunnel syndrome, and one resident even reported becoming disabled for 4 months after falling asleep at the computer and waking up with a pinched nerve in her arm. Individuals who occupy sensitive positions requiring superior health are at a particular disadvantage because their compulsive Second Life participation may cost them their job. Unfortunately, until their poor health status comes to the attention of medical staff who routinely evaluates them for safety fitness, they are at an increased risk for committing a security incident on the job.

Neglect of Work Responsibilities

Another concern is that Second Life involvement may interfere with employees' work responsibilities. Residents report experiencing addiction urges while at work, accessing the Second Life instant messaging client from work to interact with their in-world friends, being late for work, or simply not going to work because they are too tired from being in-world for 5 or more hours the night before. Residents who work from home may also experience some of these adverse consequences, because they often have Second Life running in the background when they are working. In sum, preoccupation with Second Life may serve as a major distraction for some individuals while they are trying to complete work tasks.

Discussion

Behaviors of Personnel Security Concern

The results from this ethnographic study indicate that a wide range of behaviors of potential security concern occur in Second Life. In addition, several identified behaviors raised safety and job performance concerns for all personnel, and especially for those individuals who occupy sensitive positions with health-related fitness requirements. Although the present findings describe the scope of security-relevant behaviors in Second Life, they do not indicate how often these activities occur. Planned follow-up research, as outlined in Report I, will use quantitative survey methods to assess these behaviors among users similar to security clearance holders.

Importantly, the present study found evidence that behaviors occurring in Second Life do spill over into the brick-and-mortar world. Without this connection, many of the behaviors could be dismissed as merely role-play or fantasy. Although the identified behaviors can be aligned against the Adjudicative Guidelines, they can also be understood and summarized in terms of their effects on various life domains. The behaviors that were identified can be grouped into four categories described below.

Behaviors That Can Be Used to Negatively Influence Personnel

A core concern for personnel security is that individuals might become targets for assessment, blackmail or influence by foreign or domestic agents who are trying to gather intelligence about the United States. With a small amount of detective work, they can deduce residents' real-life identities by piecing together bits of information from user profiles with information gathered through chats with them, and information from search engines such as Google. In exchange for not exposing the compromising nature of residents' behavior in Second Life, foreign agents might ask for classified information or they may try to exert influence through offers of financial rewards. The bulk of the behaviors of potential security concern either observed or reported by residents occur in this category. For the most part, they concern sexual or criminal activities, but also include contact with foreign individuals or organizations and associations with extremist groups.

An additional consideration is that extremist groups involved in hate crimes and gang activities may use Second Life to shape ideologies or recruit people to commit antigovernment or domestic terrorism actions. The atmosphere of Second Life raises long-term questions about how virtual environments will affect the ease of associations with these groups. Many residents report that the perceived anonymity of Second Life, coupled with a heightened sense of closeness to other residents and desire for self-expression, makes them feel comfortable trying out new risky behaviors and developing friendships with strangers. The most notable compromising behaviors that might expose users to influence include:

- Virtual extramarital sex.
- Age-play.
- Bestiality.
- Compromising sexual experimentation.
- Virtual sex work.
- Financial overspending.
- Contact with foreign individuals, organizations, and embassies.
- Involvement in romantic relationships with foreigners.
- Involvement in gangs or hate groups.
- Involvement in extremist groups.

Behaviors That Compromise Performance and Reliability in the Workplace

Behaviors in this category concern the relationship between participation in Second Life and workplace performance and reliability. Individuals who spend excessive time in-world, also report having a poor sleep schedule, skipping work, having a difficult time focusing on work tasks, and even attempting to access Second Life while at work. These behaviors would be a security risk for most jobs, and particularly ones demanding a superior ability to sustain cognitive focus on tasks (e.g., working with nuclear materials or weapons).

This category also includes behaviors that involve illegal computer activities and violations of personal conduct. Linden Lab's TSA clearly prohibits such behaviors as griefing, hacking, and theft of intellectual property that belongs to other residents, so individuals who abuse Second Life's IT infrastructure in-world are breaking the official rules. Per existing reporting requirements, these sorts of behaviors require investigation and adjudicative review. It is plausible that these individuals would also have a difficult time complying with IT rules and regulations in the workplace, even though the present study did not examine this question empirically. Lying is another behavior that could potentially spill over into the workplace if it becomes overly prevalent in-world, especially if individuals are poor at separating their Second Life identity from the one they uphold in real life. The major types of behaviors that may compromise performance and reliability in the workplace include:

- Absenteeism.
- Addiction urges while at work.
- Cognitive interference or "split world" effect.
- Sleep deprivation.
- Accessing Second Life or its features while at work when this behavior is prohibited.
- Hacking.
- Harassment of other Second Life residents.
- Use of illegal scripts.
- Lying.

Behaviors That Undermine Mental and Physical Health

Disturbed mental health, which falls under psychological conditions in the Adjudicative Guidelines, could cause a significant deficit to an individual's psychological, social and occupational functioning. Compulsive cyber use surfaced as one of the most prominent concerns in this category. This condition is behaviorally similar to other forms of addiction (e.g., alcohol, drugs, etc.), and in the present context involves such features as excessive use of Second Life, withdrawal symptoms when the Second Life access is inaccessible, build-up of tolerance including the need for more hours in-world, and negative social and occupational consequences. It cannot be concluded that Second Life residents in the present study met the clinical criteria for an impulse control disorder, but they certainly exhibited the symptoms of this condition.

Behaviors associated with undermined physical health are also grouped into this category. While not a security risk, poor physical health may be a safety risk for certain sensitive positions with additional requirements. Also, neglect of physical health indicates poor judgment on the part of individuals who spend extended periods of time in-world, despite experiencing strain on their back, neck, and hands, and neglecting a proper diet, exercise, and maintenance of personal hygiene. The primary types of behaviors that undermine mental and physical health include:

- Anxiety attacks.
- Compulsive cyber use.
- Paranoia.
- Reduced guard.
- Back and neck strain.
- Carpal tunnel syndrome.
- Neglect of diet.
- Neglect of exercise.
- Neglect of personal hygiene.

Behaviors That Interfere with Real-world Functioning and Relationships

The final category of concerns addresses relationships with friends, coworkers, and family members. Findings from the present study show that problematic Second Life involvement can break up relationships and marriages and result in neglect of spouses, children, and friends. It is of potential concern that over time some individuals may start replacing their real-world connections with virtual connections and fully disconnect from society. Their real-life emotional safety net may diminish in favor of one that is not reliable.

Moreover, replacement of real-world connections with virtual connections will likely result in increased amounts of time spent in-world, which introduces additional security risks such as cyber addiction and involvement in behaviors that could make individuals vulnerable to outside influence. The list of behaviors that interfere with real-world functioning and relationships is presented below:

- Replacing real-world families with Second Life families.
- Betraying real-world romantic partners by forming cyber relationships.
- Neglecting real-world children.
- Disconnecting from real-world friends.
- Using Second Life as an escape from real-world problems.
- Forming unrealistic expectations regarding real emotional connections.

Conclusions and Implications

The relative newness of Second Life and similar environments, along with the general focus of the personnel security culture on managing threats, may leave the impression that Second Life participation only has negative effects. However, a great many of in-world activities encourage social awareness, acceptance of other cultures, and development of real-world interpersonal skills. Per residents' feedback, the social skills acquired in Second Life may even transfer into real-world situations, such as in the case of shy individuals who start practicing being extroverted in real life. Finally, regardless of potential personnel security concerns, trying risky behaviors in a fantasy context may be preferable to acting them out in real life.

Importantly, Second Life participation is likely to have a different impact on ordinary users versus those who are eligible for access to classified information Non-clearance holders need not be concerned with the potential security risks of their in-world activities, only how they might undermine realistic human relationships and lead to poor personal or employment outcomes. On the whole, Second Life is an alternative to other forms of entertainment or creative expression, and can provide an escape from the mundane reality, pressures, and obligations of real life (Boellstorff, 2008). Clearance holders, on the other hand, may be placing themselves at risk when they engage in various behaviors that surfaced in the present ethnography. For them, the prospective benefits may not necessarily outweigh the costs, at least from a risk management perspective. Of course, the level of risk would be determined by the precise nature of their Second Life activities and the surrounding circumstances, and will vary on case by case basis.

A long-term goal, in conjunction with the forthcoming additional research, is to generate clear guidance for the patterns of cyber participation and specific activities that may be of concern during background investigations and continuing evaluation of current employees, and patterns of behavior viewed as safe and acceptable. Such a document would be valuable to prospective clearance applicants, current clearance holders, investigators, and adjudicators. Before any form of adverse actions related to participation are taken, it is necessary to have clear and complete training materials that detail which behaviors must be avoided, and how people can recognize warning signs in themselves and in their co-workers.

SECTION 2: CASE STUDIES

Method

Overview

The case studies presented below are based on a series of one-on-one interviews with 10 respondents who consented to being interviewed in real life. Roughly half of these individuals also participated in voice interviews and were then selected for the case studies because they reported behaviors that warranted a deeper understanding due to being potential security risks. The other respondents participated in discussion groups and numerous prior conversations with the researchers and were selected for their willingness to openly and honestly talk about their Second Life involvement and its influence on their real life. Researchers took great care to ensure that the final sample of participants was diverse regarding gender, age, occupation, socio-economic status, and United States geographical region.

The respondents were interviewed in public locations with low levels of noise located in their own towns of residence (e.g., coffee shop, public library, etc.). Researchers used an open-ended, semistructured field guide to direct the flow of the interviews (see Appendix D). This format was chosen because it provides a way for participants to describe the influence of Second Life on various aspects of their life in their own words, while at the same time covering all topics of interest. The topics included many domains of personal functioning, such as early childhood, daily activities, work life, family life, health issues, etc. The primary objectives of the face-to-face interviews were to understand how the respondents came to engage in potentially risky in-world behaviors and what impact these behaviors had on various aspects of their life. The interviews lasted approximately two hours and each respondent was paid $300 U.S. for participation.

Participants

Ten individuals were interviewed for the present study. Respondents' demographic characteristics are listed below:

- **Gender**: Six males and four females.
- **Age Range**: 22 to 62 years old.
- **Geographic Location**: The West Coast, Great Plains, Midwest, Northeast, and Southwest.

- **Area of Residence**: Rural, small city, suburban, and metropolitan areas.
- **Employment**: Seven full-time employees, three self-employed.
- **Occupation**: IT services for federal government, program manager for state government, teacher, customer service representative, computer programmer, graphic artist, social worker, public policy activist, green services installer, education team member for a technology company.
- **Economic Strata**: Lower class to upper-middle class.
- **Marital Status**: Three single and never married, five married, two divorced and engaged to someone else.

Interviews

Each interview consisted of three phases that occurred in the following order:

1) **Main interview:** A semi-structured interview was conducted, whereby the field guide was used to focus on topics of concern for each participant and skip over those that were irrelevant. They researcher introduced probing open-ended questions, and then allowed the respondent to talk freely without interruption. Follow-up questions were asked if needed for clarification. The main interview took up the majority of the 2 hour period.
2) **Quote response:** When the main interview was complete, the researcher read 20 particularly salient quotes gathered during the earlier group discussions and voice interviews (e.g., "It is very easy for me to lose time in Second Life," "I am totally ashamed of Second Life," " I don't trust anyone, but nowadays it isn't keeping me from communicating with people"). Each participant was asked to respond to each quote, first for personal relevance, or if it did not apply, then for general thoughts on the topic. Participants' responses to the quotes were then used in the analysis as an indicator of comfort level with talking about personal experiences versus distancing themselves by talking about generalities or the experiences of other residents.
3) **Written exercise:** The third and final component of the interview consisted of a written exercise. Respondents were given a blank sheet of paper and asked to write a brief description of how they perceived themselves. The instructions were intentionally left fairly open to

encourage self-expression. They were also informed that their responses would not be read until a later time.

Summary of Results

Overview

This section presents an abbreviated version of each case study and an overview of all major findings and conclusions. Although no PII was intentionally collected from any of the respondents, in order to protect their anonymity and confidentiality, only the For Official Use Only (FOUO) version of this report contains the full-length case studies. The present general release version contains only the summaries that reflect the most essential facts and an overview of the conclusions. The FOUO version of the report also contains a more nuanced discussion section that references specific case studies where deemed appropriate. All conclusions about the impact of Second Life involvement on respondents' lives are based solely on researchers' qualitative data analyses. No attempt was made to verify these conclusions by conducting additional interviews with family members, friends, and co-workers. When reviewing the case studies, the reader may find it helpful to refer to the glossary of common Second Life terms provided in Appendix A.

Case Study # 1: "Jack"

Jack experienced a rough childhood and adolescence, followed by a series of jobs in various industries, and then eventually a career in IT services. He is very dissatisfied with his current job however, because of how little it pays. He blames the economic downturn for having to take a low paying job with the federal government. He admits to experiencing anger problems at work, and at times even intimidating personnel by threatening that he will disable their accounts if they don't strictly abide by the rules.

Jack spends his time in Second Life interacting with individuals who work at mainstream defense and technology-oriented organizations and other places that he respects. Jack has used alts for social experiments to see if he can manipulate other Second Life users and has also experimented with female avatars. He loves the fact that he can try out different personalities in Second Life and disguise his real-life introversion. Jack has a strained relationship with his wife and feels little emotional connection with others both in-world and in real life. He shares a wealth of personal information about himself in his profile, such that his real-life identity can be easily deduced.

Case Study # 2: "William"

William describes himself as utterly miserable in his real life. He has grown bored with his predictable life at home, so he turns to Second Life for added excitement. He is also unhappy at work and feels that his manager makes his life a nightmare. In addition to being an avid Second Life user, William has several real-life hobbies that he regularly pursues.

Second Life serves a highly social function for William. When in-world, he focuses on friendships and relationships he's developed there. His loves the anonymity aspect, because it allows him to open up to others in-world and escape from his unhappy real life. In Second Life, he is engaged to a woman whom he describes as "a very nice lady." He admits to having a lot of virtual sex with her and says that they are going to get married in-world. William's wife does not know about her existence, and he does his best to keep his Second Life involvement a secret from everyone in his real life. He has a good reason to do so, because his job demands a high level of conscientiousness from him, and his career would be compromised had others found out about his specific activities in Second Life.

Case Study # 3: "Robert"

Robert had a rough childhood and adolescence, which included drugs, criminal activities, and run-ins with the law. He credits prison with saving his life and inspiring him to earn a Master's degree. Right now he has a stable and well-paying job. Robert is a big fan of gaming and computing and recalls joining Second Life shortly after its initial launch. He makes his real-life identity transparent in-world and is only interested in befriending those who adhere to the same policy. His pet peeve is when other users try to deceive him, so he goes to great lengths to verify the information they share with him. Second Life is very much a social community for Robert, and he is engaged to be married to someone in-world.

Robert has tried his hand at various Second Life activities, some involving large amounts of money spent on goods and services or on financial assistance given to his in-world friends—all of which he dismisses as discretionary spending. He has also tried out alternative sexual practices such as BDSM, but didn't find them fulfilling. Eventually, he turned to building and writing scripts allowing him to monitor the movements of other avatars, discover IP addresses, and design his own sims. He finds building and scripting gratifying because it gives him complete control over his Second Life environment. He has been suspended from Second Life before for rule breaking, but his account was subsequently reactivated by Linden Lab. Robert perceives his real-life self as unattractive and unappealing to others, so he credits Second Life with allowing him to enjoy a perfectly crafted life, filled with attention from others, especially attractive women.

Case Study # 4: "Maria"

Maria experienced a lot of emotional trauma as a child and teenager, which taught her to be distrustful of other people. She has also experienced physical problems that made her feel insecure about her appearance. After a number of years, she has finally pulled her personal life and career together and feels content with her life. Maria's initial experience with Second Life involved shadowing a friend who was engaged in age-play, but she made a conscious decision to disconnect from him and his group of friends and re-enter in the form of an avatar closely resembling her real-life self. Maria's current activities in Second Life are laid back and "clean fun," as she describes them.

Maria was previously involved in a long-term romantic relationship with a man from another country who ended up lying to her frequently while they were together and in the end showed no interest in moving the relationship into real life. Maria's current relationship, also with a man she met online, has bled over into real life, which makes her very happy. Despite her disappointing online experiences from the past, Maria likes Second Life because it protects her emotions by giving her the option to withdraw from relationships and friendships if somebody breaks her trust. She feels in complete control of her environment and her associates, and she is able to try out behaviors that run counter to her real-life personality, such as being extroverted and confident. She does admit to being overly trusting of others in Second Life in the past, but claims she has learned from those mistakes.

Case Study # 5: "Joanne"

Joanne is in a stable marriage, but she and her husband have their own hobbies and schedules. Joanne is quite passionate about Second Life where she spends nearly every evening after her husband goes to bed. She is not ashamed of her Second Life involvement, and her friends and family know about it. Joanne has even tried educating her friends, family, and co-workers about unique opportunities available in Second Life. She also doesn't hide her real-life identity from others in-world, but says that people first have to earn her trust before she decides to share it with them.

Joanne spends the majority of her time in Second Life, which can amount to 30 hours a week, engaged in activities that are an extension of her real-life career or a substitute for her real-life hobbies. She has developed a large number of in-world friendships with individuals from all over the world, including the Middle East. She enjoys helping people, which explains the counseling role she has taken in many of these relationships. Joanne is quick to point out that she likes to be in control and this is something she's been struggling with her whole life. Second Life appeals to her because it allows her to be in full control of her environment and friendships.

Case Study # 6: "George"

George is a conservative man who is plagued by conflicts between his ideological beliefs and impulsive actions in both real life and Second Life. He credits Second Life with inspiring him to get involved with other forms of social media, including Facebook and Twitter. While in Second Life, George only communicates with complete strangers who he has met online. George's cyber involvement has put great strains on his marriage, and he is finding it increasingly difficult to separate between his real life and his cyber life, although he does his best to keep his cyber life a secret from his friends, extended family, and co-workers.

At one time George has experimented with certain Second Life behaviors of sexual nature that he never felt free to explore in real life. In the aftermath, he stopped doing them because he became concerned that his life would be ruined if these experiments became public. George is also not a stranger to Second Life romantic relationships, which have created much animosity and strain within his real-life marriage. He states that his current Second Life relationship is no longer sexual, and that he came to a strained understanding regarding it with his wife. He admits that he is in love with his Second Life partner, but that he is only cheating on his real-life wife "in fantasy."

Case Study # 7: "Andrew"

Andrew experienced a rocky adolescence and young adulthood filled with lack of parenting and persistent bullying in school. Because of feelings of powerlessness during his formative years, Andrew is trying to exert as much control as possible over his current life. He has always loved gaming, because it allowed him to escape a stressful family life and school abuse, which could not be controlled otherwise. He similarly loves Second Life because of the control it affords over his in-world environment.

In Second Life, Andrew is heavily involved in a sexual role-play community, and he also runs a small in-world business to fund his Second Life experience. He views Second Life as merely a game and states that he can easily separate it from his real life. In the past, Andrew has used Second Life to enhance his real-life romantic partnerships. His primary relationship dissolved, however, because his partner cheated on him. Andrew feels that in order to have a decent Second Life experience and receive the full benefits of participation, one must be willing to invest at least three hours a day to being in-world, which he consistently does himself.

Case Study # 8: "Catherine"

Having experienced a rough childhood and a tumultuous marriage, Catherine is not a stranger to verbal and physical abuse. She has made a conscious decision, however, to get her life back on track. Catherine does not separate between her real life and Second Life, although there was a time in the past when Second Life felt more real and important than her real life. She would go there to escape real-world problems in her marriage, viewing the virtual space as an outlet for forgetting about her troubles and as an apparatus for boosting her self-esteem.

Catherine's past activities in Second Life have largely involved socializing with other users, both romantic interests and friends, but she is now finding herself doing it increasingly less. A stint with romantic relationships in Second Life prompted Catherine to seek relationships in the real world through an ordinary dating website, where she met her fiancé. She felt that people in Second Life were never what they appeared to be in-world, and they were always hiding something about themselves. Although in the past Catherine felt an increased need to be in Second Life and seek out affirmation from her virtual friends, she is now more satisfied with her real-life self, and no longer turns to Second Life for reassurance.

Case Study # 9: "Laura"

Laura is a career-oriented woman who has been interested in computers, gaming, and cyber interaction for quite some time now. Her boyfriend introduced her to Second Life, which she prefers to multiplayer online games due to its greater elasticity for crafting a personalized world. Laura views Second Life as the latest tool for her to use in the evolution of computer technology to assist with personal and work projects.

Laura makes her identity transparent in-world because she says her interest in Second Life is for work-related purposes. She admits, however, to having created alts in order to escape the confines of her work-related avatar, and she takes great pains to hide these identities from her Second Life friends. Laura also says that her preoccupation with Second Life has caused some problems in her life. She has found it difficult to control the amount of money and time she spends in-world, even despite realizing that her real-life interests and priorities are getting put on the back burner.

Case Study # 10: "Edward"

Edward is a small business owner in real life. Although he started out using Second Life for work-related purposes, currently the majority of his time in-world is spent creating friendships and developing intense romantic partnerships with women. He is married in real life and does not hide his Second Life involvement from his wife. Edward uses Second Life as a tool for exploration, understanding his own personality, and finding an emotional connection that is missing from his real-life marriage. He has spent a considerable amount of money in-world at the expense of his real-life financial obligations.

Edward's real-world identity is completely transparent in Second Life. He is also very open about his romantic partnerships in and out of Second Life, and has little concern about negative repercussions from mixing the two worlds. However, Edward does have an alt for times when he feels burdened with official communication in-world and wants to behave without any inhibitions.

Conclusions and Discussion

The case studies presented in this report provide insight into the impact of Second Life involvement on respondents' real-world functioning, relationships, work life, mental health, and physical health. When drawing inferences from these findings, it is important to understand that they are intended to be rich examples of different types of Second Life users, and not all of these respondents show evidence of problematic behavior or adverse spillover. Although, half of the participants were selected for the real-world interviews precisely because their stories could shed light on spillover and other themes associated with security risk. Also, while all respondents were employed and were United States citizens, and they spanned genders, ages, income levels, and geographical regions, only one held a security clearance. There is no evidence about whether these individuals are similar to the population of active clearance holders overall. However, as the number of clearance holders and Second Life participants range into the millions, it stands to reason that some do resemble the individuals presented here.

Three key themes emerged from the case studies: (1) compulsive use, (2) diminished quality of life, and (3) preference for control. Each theme is described in detail below with particular attention devoted to its importance and relevance to personnel security.

Compulsive Use

The real-world interviews allowed researchers to gain a deeper understanding of compulsive Second Life use, which can be a security concern to the extent that it impairs individuals' judgment, reliability, and trustworthiness to handle classified information or affects their capability to perform work duties. It must be noted that the term *compulsive use* in this report refers to observed and reported symptoms of excessive or somehow problematic use of Second Life rather than a clinical diagnosis. In fact, in discussions of this topic below, the term compulsive use is used in place of cyber addiction, to ensure that the reader does not presume that interviewed respondents were clinically addicted to Second Life. The present findings show that compulsive use of Second Life is not always directly proportional to the number of hours spent in-world. Instead, it's more of a qualitative phenomenon, the impact of which is best measured by examining the individual's ability to sustain proper functioning in the brick-and-mortar world, namely in the personal and workplace domains. Therefore, someone who spends five hours a week in Second Life can be just as troubled as an individual who spends 40 hours a week in-world, if the former person has suffered equal psychosocial impairments to his or her real life. All of the respondents selected for the case studies reported at some point experiencing difficulties staying away from Second Life and/or feeling preoccupied with it when offline.

Analysis of the case study findings also identified three distinct functional roles that Second Life may play in the respondents' lives. These functional roles illustrate that individuals are attracted to Second Life for distinct reasons, some of which may be more adaptive than others. Note that the resultant framework of functional roles is based on 10 case studies, so it will require further testing and validation before it can be extrapolated to a larger population of individuals. The proposed functional roles focus on the purpose behind the individual's sustained participation in Second Life, which can fall into one of three categories: (1) using Second Life as a tool for enhancing real life, (2) using Second Life as a temporary escape from real life, and (3) using Second Life as a replacement for real life. The categories are neither orthogonal nor static. An individual can fall into more than one category at the same time (e.g., using Second Life as both a tool and as a temporary escape), and they can transition from one category into another (e.g., using Second Life as a temporary escape at first because of an illness in the family and then becoming a heavy addict and having it replace one's real life). Future research is necessary to delineate how the three groups compare in the adverse psychosocial consequences that they experience as a result of their use.

- Second Life can be used as a tool for enhancing real life in order to supplement networking, education, and career opportunities that are available there. Examples include taking a foreign language class in-world because it's free and taught by a native speaker or fulfilling a work obligation in response to a supervisor's request to advertise company products in Second Life. These individuals do not conceal their Second Life involvement from their real-life family and friends and they also make their real-life activities transparent in-world. However, there are still potential security concerns. Leakage of sensitive information can occur if individuals unintentionally share it with others in-world or if they become a target of assessment or recruitment by foreign intelligence organizations.
- Second Life can be used as a temporary escape from real life in the same way that television or a hobby provides respite from the mundane realities of everyday life. Individuals use it to alleviate boredom and many of the case study respondents felt that Second Life is much more fun and interactive than other forms of entertainment. In contrast to television watching, which is a rather passive experience, being in Second Life allows individuals to design an idealized lifestyle that they would never be able to pursue in real life. Second Life offers them an opportunity to be a part of the action and to have a hand at writing the plot. In respect to implications for compulsive use, although using Second Life as a temporary escape sounds quite benign, it can be dangerous precisely because it makes for a much more involving and captivating experience than other forms of entertainment. What starts out as a temporary escape from real life can evolve into a permanent escape mechanism and ultimately a replacement for real life.
- Second Life can be used as a replacement for real life, or a specific aspect of it, such as fulfillment of emotional or sexual needs that are missing in a real-life marriage. In this manner, some individuals create vibrant lifestyles in Second Life in order to fill a hole that exists in real life. By doing so, they manage to temporarily avoid real-life problems and issues. Unfortunately, they often remain blind to the

fact that they are only exacerbating their problems further by completely withdrawing from real-life social interactions and activities. Divorces and relationship break-ups are very common outcomes for this group of individuals whose significant others often turn to various support sources for help (e.g., Online Gamers Anonymous) only to find out that their partner is hopelessly addicted to the game and isn't willing to change his or her usage patterns. This group of individuals is most likely to spend extended hours in-world and experience psychosocial symptoms of compulsive cyber use, which may include impairments to health, performance in the workplace, and personal functioning and relationships in the real world.

Diminished Quality of Life

A second prominent theme that emerged from the case studies pertains to users' quality of life. For most of the interviewed respondents, Second Life involvement actually exerted a diminishing effect on their quality of life, although hardly anyone chose to admit this was true. In contrast, interviewed respondents stated that Second Life improved their quality of life, even when it was having negative effects on their marriage, relationships with family members and friends, financial wellbeing, and other life domains. The best way to understand these quality of life effects is to examine not what the respondents were saying but how they were saying it and what they were not saying. Many individuals may simply be in denial about the opportunity costs of Second Life involvement and refuse to acknowledge them at all costs. Not surprisingly, residents whose quality of life has suffered because of their Second Life involvement also spend the largest amount of time in-world, ranging from 20 hours to 60 hours a week. Again, however, the number of hours alone should not be used as a definitive indicator of compulsive use and spillover, but only as a potential red flag.

The primary mechanism through which Second Life affects residents' quality of life is replacement of real-world social interactions with virtual ones. This is true for both romantic and platonic relationships. Individuals replace real-world spouses with Second Life spouses (and at times even children) and real-world friends with Second Life friends. As a result, one of two things may happen. Residents either tend to abandon real-life relationships or find ways to integrate Second Life interactions with real-life relationships, still and all resulting in decreased amounts of time spent with real-life family and friends. Of course, there are also individuals who use Second Life to merely expand their real-life friendships and make connections that extend beyond the boundaries of geography. In this case, one should not expect to see diminished quality of life effects, especially if the person is finding it difficult to meet friends in real life.

Preference for Control

The ability of users to control all aspects of the experience afforded by Second Life was a topic that surfaced early on in the group discussions and voice interviews, as well as the one-on-one interviews. Nearly all respondents remarked over and over that they favored Second Life because it affords great control over the in-world lifestyle, which is impossible to do in real life. This strong preference for control may be explained by another common factor that surfaced in case study respondents' backgrounds. Nearly all of the respondents reported experiencing highly stressful events during their early childhood, albeit to varying degrees. These events included divorce, adoption, physical abuse, sexual abuse, and bullying in school. Perhaps, the respondents' desire to control every aspect of their in-world lifestyle, including physical appearance, social interactions, and activities, stems from a complete lack of control they experienced in their childhood years. Future research needs to address whether in fact there is a relationship between stressful childhood experiences and subsequent problematic use of cyber environments.

Respondents found it particularly appealing that Second Life allows them to control six aspects of their Second Life lifestyle that are listed and described below. Perhaps these domains will help researchers understand why Second Life can be so addictive and appealing to individuals.

- **Communication**: Second Life offers residents the opportunity to manage their communication with others, which according to their accounts, may be the most important element of control Second Life provides. Not only can they mute residents they don't wish to talk to, but they can also ponder and edit exactly what they choose to write to other residents. They are able to mask their true feelings and send messages that reflect only the point they wish to communicate, carefully calculating the emotional implications.
- **Anonymity**: Residents can choose to reveal as little or as much about their real-life identity as they wish. They rated control of anonymity as the second most important element of control that Second Life provides. They sometimes see this anonymity as free rein to act in ways they would never consider acting in real life, and the anonymity

gives them unspoken permission to reveal emotions and events that they would never share in real life.

- **Secrecy**: Residents also enjoy the ability to create secret alts and in this manner hide their primary Second Life identity from their Second Life friends and associates, or just control their accessibility to others in-world. They often use alts to experiment with risky behaviors and to cheat on their Second Life partners. Residents can also manipulate who is able to see they are presently online, creating a level of control over their visibility to others in-world.
- **Environment**: The ability to control everything about one's environment in-world also appeals to residents. They can change their surroundings whenever they wish, or refine one location over and over until their idea of perfection is reached. Housing is also easily manipulated, designed, changed, and built again at will, which would be challenging to do in real life.
- **Appearance**: Residents greatly enjoy manipulating all aspects of their physical appearance in Second Life, something that would be much more difficult to accomplish in real life. Many residents report not being happy with their real-life physical form because of challenges such as obesity, stutter, etc. Second Life allows them to have their idealized appearance. Residents also feel that others in Second Life tend to judge them based on their personality and not their looks.
- **Personality**: Finally, residents enjoy being able to manipulate the perceptions that others hold of their personality. Many report being introverted in real life, but frequently practicing extroverted behaviors in-world. Others report being more sexually open in-world than in real life. A resident can experiment with as many different personalities as the number of alts they have. Although this behavior cannot be called explicit lying, it certainly involves deception.

SECTION 3: PERSONAS

Method

The contracted researchers also created a typology of personas as a final and third way to synthesize the findings from the present ethnography. Others, e.g., Meadows (2008), have in the past employed similar approaches to synthesizing their observations of Second Life users. This typology assigns

Second Life residents into prototypical categories based on their pattern of Second Life use and how that participation might pose a security risk. The personas were created using the data from 35 distinct voice and real-world interviews, and must be considered preliminary at best.

First, the data from the interviews were inserted into a matrix of variables. The rows in the matrix included Second Life behaviors reported by residents and the columns included all of the Adjudicative Guidelines, except for Alcohol Consumption and Drug Involvement. The columns also included three additional variables that were judged important to the persona development process: (1) hours a week spent in-world, (2) unusual behaviors or traits observed by the researchers during the data collection process, and (3) the resident's reasons for entering Second Life.

The second step was to rate each interview respondent's Second Life behaviors in the rows of the matrix as low, medium, or high for each of the column variables. An example of the rating process is presented here. "Beth" is married with children, holds a prestigious job as an executive of a large corporation, but also is a submissive sex slave in Second Life. She spends more than 40 hours a week in-world and her Second Life master, who lives in a foreign country, sends her messages throughout the day telling her what to do when she returns to Second Life that evening. He also provides input into her real-life activities. Beth gets about four or five hours of sleep each night because she goes to bed late participating in BDSM role-play, and although her husband knows she spends a lot of time in-world, he knows very little about her specific activities.

Beth was rated as high on the Personal Conduct guideline because of her sexual activities in Second Life and because these activities would pose a great risk to her marriage, job, and social standing if discovered. She was rated as high on the Foreign Influence guideline, because she abides the requests of an apparent foreign individual who she has never met in real life. She was also rated as high on the Personal Conduct guideline because she systematically hides her Second Life sexual activities from her husband, which increases the apparent risks of blackmail or exploitation. Beth admits that her husband would not like her behavior if he became aware of it. She was rated as a low risk on the remaining guidelines. The rating process was in some ways similar to the approach that adjudicators use to determine whether a subject's behavior violates specific adjudicative guidelines.

Finally, the researchers clustered the 35 interviewed respondents into groups based on the number of low, medium, and high ratings they received, in this manner deriving five personas. The personas vary on two key dimensions: (1) the functional role that Second Life serves in the individual's life and (2) the apparent security risk posed by an individual's Second Life activities. Note that the resulting categories are abstractions and do not pertain to any specific individual contacted during the course of the study.

Results

Five personas were identified during the typology development process: Reckless Risk Takers, Escapists, Substitutes, Explorers, and Enhancers. This categorization of personas complements the functional role framework derived from the case studies in that it provides a more nuanced understanding of the specific behaviors of security concern in which individuals engage in-world. While the personas describe five general types of Second Life users observed in the present study, they do not speak to how common each type is in-world. Future planned research will address the relative frequencies of user types in Second Life and also examine user types in other cyber environments. The personas are listed in descending order from highest level of potential security risk to lowest as per the concerns outlined in the Adjudicative Guidelines.

Reckless Risk Takers

Reckless Risk Takers take risks in Second Life, both in terms of the potential harm to their own health and functioning, and the potential damage to their outside lives if others find out about their activities. The signs of their Second Life involvement may not be directly visible to those around them, because Reckless Risk Takers are good at keeping secrets from families and coworkers regarding their Second Life activities. They also spend the greatest amount of time in-world compared to other personas. Due to the nature and extent of their participation, Reckless Risk Takers have a high apparent risk for blackmail or coercion.

- Reckless Risk Takers easily fall prey to outside influence, as they sometimes allow others not only to direct their lives in-world, but also at work and at home. They may also let their Second Life activities spill over into their real life, without realizing the harmful impact on their health, well-being, and relationships with family members and friends.
- Reckless Risk Takers frequently participate in explicit and non-mainstream sexual behaviors in Second Life, potentially increasing

the risk of blackmail and putting their real-life image at risk if these activities were discovered.

- Reckless Risk Takers are highly likely to overextend themselves financially in Second Life either by overspending on their Second Life lifestyle or by providing monetary assistance to other residents who claim they are in need of help.
- Reckless Risk Takers may exhibit symptoms of compulsive use by becoming increasingly dependent on Second Life over time and needing more and more time in-world to satisfy their cravings. They may deny this addiction by saying that Second Life is just a game, contradicting earlier statements that the emotions and feelings they experience in Second Life are very real.
- Reckless Risk Takers are at an increased risk for trusting other anonymous Second Life residents and sharing with them real-life personally identifying information, at times without awareness.
- If Reckless Risk Takers possess computer programming knowledge, they are at an increased risk for abusing the Linden Lab TSA and engaging in prohibited computer activities, including abuse of other residents.
- Reckless Risk Takers spend the greatest amount of time in Second Life, averaging between 30 to 60 hours per week.

Escapists

Escapists use Second Life to avoid their real-life problems. They neglect themselves, their families, and jobs and use Second Life much like a functional alcoholic uses alcohol. They may be seeking escape from a bad marriage, a meaningless social life, or a miserable job. Escapists may be most easily influenced by others when they are more emotionally vulnerable.

- Escapists are less likely to fall prey to outside influence than Reckless Risk Takers and to allow their Second Life activities to bleed over into real life. They realize that Second Life provides only a relative sense of anonymity, so they are somewhat more cautious about sharing their real-life personal information with other residents.
- Although Escapists also partake in experimental sexual behaviors, they are more likely than Reckless Risk Takers to have other interests in Second Life, including friendships with other residents and active involvement in interest groups. They tend to be somewhat more open about Second Life with their real-life family, friends, and coworkers.

- Escapists also overextend themselves financially in-world, but only to purchase Linden dollars in support of their Second Life lifestyle. They do not give real-life money to other Second Life residents.
- Escapists are better able to balance Second Life and real life than Reckless Risk Takers, for while they develop emotional ties in-world, they are motivated to protect and preserve their real-life relationships too.
- Escapists only share personal information with those they trust. The inability to verify identities within Second Life may increase their vulnerability for disclosing sensitive information, however, as social engineering may be used to gain trust.
- Escapists with computer knowledge have a medium risk of engaging in prohibited computer activities.
- Escapists spend an average of 30 hours a week in Second Life.

Substitutes

Substitutes use Second Life as a substitute for hobbies, television, or even sexual "kinks" that are not being satisfied in real life. For them, Second Life simply replaces other forms of entertainment. They are not trying to avoid real-life problems, time schedules, or obligations. A potential security risk may emerge if a Substitute replaces real-life emotional connections with unrealistic virtual relationships or if another party is a foreign national.

- Substitutes are not as easily influenced in-world and, because their real lives tend to be basically satisfying, they tend to separate Second Life from real life more than Reckless Risk Takers or Escapists.
- Substitutes experiment with sexual behaviors, but much more discreetly, and they often create an alt just for that purpose. Substitutes also frequently abandon their alts because they don't find them satisfying, or because they are busy with their other Second Life pursuits.
- Substitutes are at a moderate risk for spending excessively in-world, but tend to eliminate real-world costs (e.g., buying coffee) to offset the expenditures.
- Substitutes sometimes become immersed in Second Life at the expense of real-life friendships, and can be dishonest through alts and lies in their profiles. They are, however, less likely than Reckless Risk Takers and Escapists to abandon their family and friends. They say

they lie to protect their real-life identity rather than for personal gain or deceit.

- Substitutes are at a moderate risk for sharing sensitive information, particularly if they are trying to fill a void in real-life emotional ties, such as with a loveless marriage. If they are using Second Life as a substitute for entertainment, then the risk for exposing information is low.
- Substitutes with computer knowledge have a low risk of engaging in prohibited computer activities.
- Substitutes tend to spend an average of 25 hours a week in-world.

Explorers

Explorers use Second Life to discover and participate in experiences that are not readily accessible in real life. They are less likely to fall prey to outside influence because they primarily focus on exploring an immediate interest (e.g., building objects, listening to music, learning about other countries, finding a real-life romantic partner, etc.). They perceive Second Life as a tool for exploratory goals.

- Explorers are not likely to fall prey to outside influence. Their focus is on the task at hand.
- Explorers may try out new sexual behaviors in-world, but it is either fleeting experimentation or not something hidden from others in the real world.
- Explorers are at a moderate risk for spending excessively, but as with Substitutes, they control their entertainment budget by cutting back in other areas.
- Explorers are in-world for discovering new experiences and exploring aspects of their identity. The potential for compulsive use will therefore depend on the nature of their specific activities. They are, however, unlikely to abandon real-life relationships in favor of ones developed in Second Life, unless their level of use.
- Explorers are at a low risk for revealing personal information, and are less likely to have many social contacts in-world. They understand that others in Second Life are not honest for a variety of reasons, and are vigilant about keeping themselves protected from possible harm.
- Explorers with computer knowledge may break rules (e.g., exploring the possibilities of hacking into IT systems). They are primarily

interested, however, in learning the "hows" behind such activities than actually engaging in them.

- Explorers tend to average 15 to 20 hours a week in-world.

Enhancers

Enhancers use Second Life as a tool for work, business, and hobbies. They are the least likely of all residents to engage in compulsive use of Second Life or engage in behaviors that could be somehow used against them. They use Second Life because it helps them perform real-life activities more efficiently, and are primarily focused on that purpose. They also spend the least amount of time in Second Life relative to other personas.

- Enhancers are not likely be influenced by others, and will avoid those who try to manipulate them. They do not like to be distracted from their goals.
- Enhancers do not engage in sexual experimentation in Second Life.
- Enhancers have a very low risk for excessive spending in Second Life, as many have chosen it as a cheaper alternative to other methods of completing real-world tasks.
- Enhancers are at a low risk for becoming compulsive users of Second Life, and their outside relationships are largely unaffected by their involvement in Second Life.
- Enhancers are unlikely to share personal or sensitive information with anyone they meet in Second Life.
- Whether or not they possess computer knowledge, Enhancers are unlikely to violate the Linden Lab TSA.
- Enhancers tend to spend the least amount of time in Second Life, averaging 5 to 10 hours a week. This estimate excludes those who are required to use Second Life to complete job tasks, and only refers to usage as a productivity tool for hobbies and personal interests.

Discussion

These personas are meant to provide initial insight into differentiating between innocuous and problematic use of Second Life among current and potential clearance holders. This classification framework represents the first known attempt to evaluate participation in the context of the Adjudicative

Guidelines. Subsequently, alternative analytical frameworks are worth exploring and may provide more clear and actionable guidance. There are many parallels between virtual social environments such as Second Life and other cyber contexts (e.g., multiplayer online games, social networks, etc.) so it would be advisable to examine whether the same or different classification schemes apply to each one.

Reckless Risk Takers pose the highest level of security risk due to their involvement in sexual activities and susceptibility to outside influence. As they are typically secretive about their Second Life activities, they may be undetectable during investigations. Escapists present a moderate security risk. While their behavior resembles that of Reckless Risk Takers, their participation may be temporary and dependent on real-life satisfaction. Substitutes represent some degree of security concern, depending on their specific activities and relationships. Explorers and Enhancers provide little reason for security concern. Enhancers, in particular, are in-world to use Second Life as a tool for being more productive in their real life and are unlikely to be distracted by many of the behaviors associated with high levels of security risk.

The developed typology of personas only describes the different types of Second Life users who were interviewed for the purposes of the present ethnography. No information is currently available on the frequency of each user type in the population of all Second Life users or in the population of all potential and current clearance holders. Also, it is impossible to firmly assess the security risk associated with each persona with the methods used in this study, and further research is necessary. Two other interesting research areas need to be examined further: (1) the relative stability of each persona, and (2) the situational factors (e.g., goals, life circumstances, and personality factors) that predict which persona a Second Life user will adopt. Both of these topics are important because Second Life personas are not static. Participation ebbs and flows for individual Second Life residents and someone can start out as one persona and evolve into another depending upon multiple factors in their real lives. That is because certain real-life challenges and personality characteristics can make individuals more susceptible to behaviors of concern in Second Life, and they can compel them to progress from one persona to another. Interviews with study participants show that these factors may include:

- **Death of a spouse or a loved one**, where involvement in Second Life is a way to distract oneself from the grieving process and replace the emotional connection that is no longer present.
- **Taking care of a sick spouse or parent** can leave individuals feeling unappreciated, alone, and stressed out. Second Life provides them with a temporary relief without making them feel guilty for leaving the person alone at home.
- **Divorce** can cause low self-esteem, compelling the individual to either hide behind the computer screen or to seek out reassurance online in an attempt to prevent being hurt again by keeping romantic partners at a distance.
- **Low self-esteem**, in particular as it relates to self-perceptions of attractiveness can prompt someone to create an unrealistically attractive avatar and hide behind him or her. Individuals report choosing this route because they are hoping that someone will become so attracted to their personality that their real-life physical appearance will not matter.
- **Personality traits** such as introversion can make individuals feel more comfortable developing friendships and romantic partnerships in Second Life as opposed to in the real world.

The framework of personas can also be understood in the context of the functional roles that Second Life serves for its users. Recall that individuals can use Second Life as a tool for enhancing real life, as a temporary escape from real life, or replacement for their real life. Figure 3 illustrates how personas fit into this functional role framework. Specifically, Reckless Risk Takers and Escapists use Second Life either as an escape from their real life or as a replacement for it. The nature of their risky behavior in-world puts them at a risk for becoming unfit for safeguarding classified information. For Substitutes, Second Life fulfills the role of an escape from their real life, in the form of a thrilling entertainment tool analogous to the television, but much more captivating. Explorers use Second Life to either escape their real life or as a tool to enhance it. It is important to examine the nature of their specific activities in-world to understand whether they are a security risk. Finally, Enhancers use Second Life exclusively as a tool for enhancing their real life and they are at a very low risk for engaging in behaviors that will make them unreliable or somehow undermine their judgment.

In conclusion, it is always vital to examine (1) the situational factors prevalent in the individual's life, (2) personality characteristics, and (3) the specific nature of Second Life activities when trying to estimate the degree of security risk stemming from the individual's Second Life involvement. These characteristics should be examined in conjunction with the functional role that Second Life fulfills for the individual and the persona that best characterizes his or her behavior in-world.

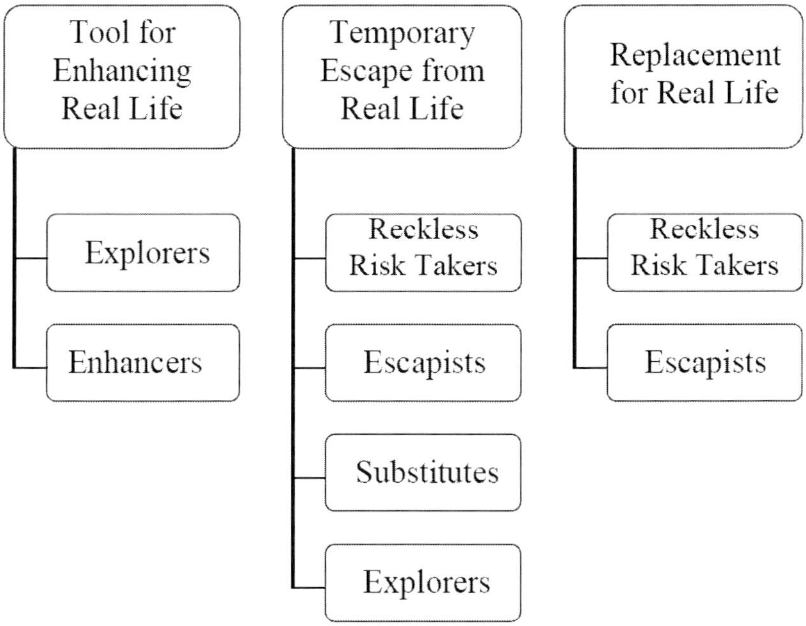

Figure 3. The Relationship Between Second Life Functional Roles and Personas.

SECTION 4: GENERAL DISCUSSION AND RECOMMENDATIONS

Overview

This report, as the second in an ongoing series of PERSEREC's Cyber Culture and Personnel Security projects, provides initial information about behaviors of personnel security concern occurring in Second Life and outlines their apparent impact on users' physical and mental health, work life, relationships, and functioning in the real world. Although Second Life lacks the physical contact of real life, it provides an alternative environment for the occurrence of nearly all concerns outlined in the Adjudicative Guidelines. Importantly for the personnel security community, virtual behaviors are unlikely to emerge during a background investigation as many users tend to be secretive about their Second Life activities and the Standard Form 86 (SF-86) does not ask about cyber involvement.

The real challenge is that behavior in virtual environments can spill over into the brick-and-mortar world and impact an employee's reliability, judgment, and trustworthiness in the workplace. Unfortunately, individuals are often unaware of the changes to their normal behavior introduced by cyber participation (Aboujaoude, 2011). The present research is a first attempt at understanding virtual social environments, in the form of (1) which behaviors of potential personnel security concern occur, (2) detailed case studies that illustrate the motivations of users and the real-world impact of participation, and (3) initial personas that describe patterns of innocuous versus problematic use. The remaining portion of this report summarizes the key findings from the present ethnography and provides initial recommendations for personnel security professionals and policy makers. Subsequent Cyber Culture and Personnel Security reports will provide actionable recommendations for how to address participation in virtual social environments during investigative, adjudicative, and continuous evaluation phases.

Summary of Main Findings

A number of Second Life behaviors raised security concerns about the judgment, reliability, and trustworthiness of individuals who participate in them. In addition, a number of the identified behaviors dealt with personnel's overall job performance and fitness to occupy sensitive positions with additional physical and cognitive health requirements (e.g., Department of Energy's Human Reliability Program positions). The prevalence rate of these behaviors is presently unknown and will be examined in a quantitative study summarized in future research. The behaviors that were identified can (1) be used to negatively influence personnel, (2) compromise performance and reliability in the workplace, (3) undermine mental and physical health, and (4) interfere with real-world functioning and relationships.

A set of case studies was developed on the basis of extensive one-on-one interviews with a subset of the participants who met with researchers in real life. These case studies provide insight into the impact of Second Life involvement on respondents' real-world functioning, relationships, work life, mental health, and physical health. Specifically, they suggest that individuals can use Second Life as (1) a tool for enhancing their real life, (2) a temporary escape from real life, and (3) a replacement for real life. Generally, only the third type of usage might generate concerns about potential clinical addiction, withdrawal from real-life social interactions and activities, and undermined health. Interviews with case study respondents also revealed that problematic use should not be measured in strictly quantitative terms (i.e., the number of hours), but rather understood in terms of the broader impact of cyber involvement on the person's functioning in the brick-and-mortar world. Finally, the majority of interviewed respondents exhibited a strong preference for control, which they felt Second Life allowed them to satisfy.

The present ethnography also resulted in development of an initial framework for distinguishing between innocuous use of no apparent security concern from problematic use that may pose risks to national security. Specifically, it identified five unique personas that best capture and describe the wide range of Second Life users: Reckless Risk Takers, Escapists, Substitutes, Explorers, and Enhancers. Reckless Risk Takers pose the highest level of security risk due to their involvement in sexual activities and susceptibility to outside influence. As they are typically secretive about their Second Life activities, they may be undetectable during investigations, especially since SF-86 does not ask questions about cyber involvement. Future testing and validation of this framework is necessary, as it does not speak to the relative frequencies of each persona type or to whether it applies to other cyber environments.

Recommendations

This research contains implications for revising the personnel security vetting and continuous evaluation process in three important ways:

1) **Update Definition of Contact in Adjudicative Guidelines**. The national Adjudicative Guidelines currently focus exclusively on behaviors that occur in the real world, without recognizing that the cyber world is a ripe context for nearly all of the adverse behaviors described in the guidelines. The cyber world may lack the physical contact component present in real life, but the lives that individuals build and lead in virtual worlds such as Second Life have very real

consequences for their health, job performance, and real-world functioning. It is time to reevaluate the importance of physical contact for the purposes of defining a behavior as adverse, and also update the SF-86, the investigative standards, and the adjudicative guidelines to reflect the most up to date understanding of security risk that stems from involvement in virtual realities.

2) **Educate Personnel How to Avoid Risks.** The findings from this research can also serve as an educational tool for personnel who desire to participate in virtual realities, but do not understand the potential risks of these environments for their workplace and real-life functioning. Personnel education can be accomplished by providing informational materials or developing an online training module that will describe the potential risks of virtual involvement for employees' performance in the workplace, physical and mental health, and real-life functioning. The training materials should also provide strategies for how to avoid these risks and participate in virtual realities in a safe and productive manner.
3) **Implement Peer Reporting Systems.** Problematic cyber involvement in virtual realities may be difficult to detect through self-report or automated cyber vetting, so peer reporting may play a vital role in bringing it to light. Personnel should therefore be taught how to distinguish signs of maladaptive cyber use from routine or healthy cyber involvement in their colleagues and how to appropriately report these indicators. Previous research has shown that employees are reluctant to report coworker behavior that isn't directly associated with national security (Wood & Marshall-Mies, 2003), and without adequate education, cyber use may fall into this category. Personnel education will therefore be a crucial first step before peer reporting can be successfully implemented.

These three initial recommendations are based on the findings from the present ethnography, and additional actionable recommendations for policymakers, investigators, and adjudicators will be provided in forthcoming Cyber Culture and Personnel Security reports. This planned research will use quantitative survey methods to assess how frequently behaviors of security concern actually occur in the workforce similar to clearance holders in both Second Life and in the other major categories of cyber environments (e.g., online multiplayer games, social networks, etc.).

REFERENCES

Aboujaoude, E. (2011). *Virtually you: The dangerous powers of e-personality.* New York, NY: W.W. Norton & Company.

Bardzell, S. (2006). The submissive speaks: The semiotics of visuality in virtual BDSM fantasy play. *Proceedings of the 2006 ACM SIGGRAPH Symposium on Videogames, 99-102.* New York, NY: ACM Press.

Barfield, T. (1997). *The dictionary of anthropology.* Malden, MA: Blackwell Publishing.

Boellstorff, T. (2008). *Coming of age in Second Life.* Princeton, NJ: Princeton University Press.

Castronova, E. (2005). *Synthetic worlds: The business and culture of online games.* Chicago, IL: University of Chicago Press.

Castronova, E. (2007). *Exodus to the virtual world: How online fun is changing reality.* New York, NY: Palgrave Macmillan.

Ervin, A. M. (2000). *Applied anthropology: Tools and perspectives for contemporary practice.* Needham Heights, MA: Allyn & Bacon.

Herbig, K. L. (2008). *Changes in espionage by Americans: 1947-2007* (TR 08-05). Monterey, CA: Defense Personnel Security Research Center.

IACP. (2010). *Developing a cybervetting strategy for law enforcement.* Alexandria, VA: International Association of Chiefs of Police.

Jenkins, H. (2010). Watching the watchers: Power and politics in Second Life. Retrieved March 1, 2010, from http://www.convergenceculture.org /weblog/2010/04/watching_the_watche rs_power_an.php

Kehoe, J. F. (2009). *Examination of the adjudicative guidelines.* Office of the Director of National Intelligence.

Leggitt, J. S., Shechter, O. G., & Lang, E. L. (Tech. Rpt. 11-01). *Cyber culture and personnel security: Report I – orientation, concerns and needs.* Monterey, CA: Defense Personnel Security Research Center.

Linden Lab. (2007). Clarification of policy disallowing "ageplay." Retrieved March 1, 2010, from http://blogs /blog/2007/11/14/clarific ation-of-policy-disallowing-ageplay

Linden Lab. (2010a). Terms of Service. Retrieved March 1, 2010, from http://secondlife.com/corporate/tos.php

Linden Lab. (2010b). Linden Lab official: An overview of Second Life security. Retrieved March 13, 2010, from http://wiki.secondlife.com /wiki/Linden_Lab_Official:An_Overview_of_Secon d_Life_Security

MaxMind. (2008). GeoIP. (Version 1.7). [Computer software]. Waltham, MA: MaxMind.

Meadows, M. S. (2008). *I, avatar: The culture and consequences of having a Second Life*. Berkeley, CA: New Riders Press.

Mennecke, B. E., McNeill, D., Roche, E. M., Bray, D. A., Townsend, A. M., & Lester, J. (2008). Second Life and other virtual worlds: A roadmap for research. *Communications of the Association for Information Systems, 22,* 371-388.

Reuters, E. (2008). Virtual retailers decry Second Life crime wave. Retrieved May 30, 2010, from http://secondlife.reuters.com/stories/2008/02/07 /virtualretailers-decry-second-life-crime-wave/index.html

Taylor, T. L. (2006). *Play between worlds: Exploring online game culture.* Cambridge, MA: MIT Press.

Wood, S., & Marshall-Mies, J. C. (2003). *Improving supervisor and coworker reporting of information of security concern.* (TR 02-3). Monterey, CA: Defense Personnel Security Research Center.

Appendix A: Glossary of Second Life Terms

Glossary of Second Life Terms

Alt: An alternate or additional avatar that complements a Second Life resident's primary avatar. An alt is often created for the purpose of trying out taboo behaviors not wanted to be associated with the user's primary avatar.

Avatar: A moveable, three-dimensional visual representation of the user's identity in cyberspace. In Second Life, most avatars are male or female humans, but any sort of object can be used. They are also sometimes called a "character."

Avie: Abbreviated form of the term "avatar" frequently used in Second Life.

BDSM: The compound acronym of several sexual references that stands for Bondage, Discipline, Domination, & Submission (BDSM). The BDSM culture is based upon a consensual, sexual tension that is derived from intentionally unequal sexual roles: The dominant role (also called tops, dominants, or dominatrix) and the submissive role (also called bottoms or subs).

Bestiality: A behavior that involves attraction and/or sexual contact with animals. In cyber environments, such as Second Life, the sexual contact is simulated. Second Life members who are a part of this culture take steps to protect the locations where they meet to engage in zoophytical acts.

Dom: Abbreviated form of the term "dominant."

Dominant: An individual in a BDSM relationship that assumes the commanding position.

Furry Culture: A real life and Second Life culture that consists of people, known colloquially as "furries," who possess both animal and human characteristics. Furries generally most closely resemble humans wearing animal costumes rather than animals. Members of this culture interact for both sexual and nonsexual purposes.

Griefer: Someone who partakes in griefing.

Griefing: A Second Life term for harassment or pulling pranks on others. Griefing can often be malicious or systematic and certain forms are banned in Second Life. Examples of griefing include using third-party hacking programs, insulting and intimidating other residents, trying to steal property belonging to others, etc.

In-world: Occurring in Second Life.

IM: An acronym referring to the act of receiving and sending instant messages and communicating via instant messenger online chat. Instant messaging involves the act of text-based communication between two or more people using personal computers or other devices.

Newb: Abbreviated form of the term "newbie."

Newbie: An often derogatory term used to identify new residents in Second Life who are perceived to be ignorant about the rules, customs, culture, and inner workings of the virtual world. Newbies are often duped and preyed on by griefers or others with a specific agenda.

Persona: An archetypal category label that describes a Second Life resident's personality and behavior in-world by placing him or her in a typology of representative users.

Resident: A culturally preferred alternative term of reference for a user of Second Life.

Second Life: Generally accepted to be the most popular, diverse, and well-known 3D virtual environment that allows its users or residents to communicate, share experiences, and build user-created content.

Sim: A term used by Second Life residents to refer to a specific location or region in-world.

Sub: Abbreviated form of the term "submissive."

Submissive: A person in a BDSM relationship that assumes the obedient role.

APPENDIX B: PARTICIPANT SCREENING QUESTIONNAIRE

Participant Screening Questionnaire

1. Have you participated in any research studies in the last six months?

[ ] No
[ ] Yes

2. What is your age?

[ ] under 18
[ ] 18 or older

3. Of what countries or country are you a citizen?

[ ] United States
[ ] Multiple countries
[ ] Any other country

4. What is your current employment status?

[ ] Student
[ ] Self-employed
[ ] Employed full-time
[ ] Looking for work
[ ] Stay-at-home mom or dad
[ ] Unemployed and not seeking work
[ ] I make most of my real-life income in Second Life

5. Have you held, currently hold, or would you consider holding a job that requires a background investigation (this includes jobs like teachers, government employees, pilots, bank tellers, and more)?

[ ] No
[ ] Yes

6. On a scale of 1 to 10, how would you rate your real-life socioeconomic status from 1 being poor to 10 being wealthy?

(POOR) 1 2 3 4 5 6 7 8 9 10 (RICH)
(MIDDLE CLASS)

7. What is your real-life gender?

[ ] Female
[ ] Male

8. What is your real-life marital status?

[ ] Married
[ ] Single
[ ] Divorced
[ ] Widowed

9. How often are you in Second Life?

[ ] 5 hours a month or less
[ ] At least 5 hours week
[ ] About 10 to 20 hours a week
[ ] About 20 hours a week or more

10. How long have you been a resident of Second Life?

[ ] Less than three months
[ ] About three months or more

11. Where do you most often spend your Second Life time?

[ ] Hanging out by myself in crowded places
[ ] In group activities like role-playing, classes, or formal groups
[ ] Hanging out with friends I've made in Second Life
[ ] Exploring Second Life by myself

APPENDIX C: SPONSORED GROUP DISCUSSIONS AND VOICE INTERVIEW FIELD GUIDE

This field guide was used to direct the flow of questions asked during sponsored group discussions and voice interviews. It consists of open-ended question probes organized around the topical areas of Adjudicative Guidelines A-F and I-M (e.g., cultural identity, financial influences, psychological conditions, etc.). Note that the questions in the field guide are organized around cultural focus areas instead of specific guidelines. This structure is necessary in order to create a more natural flow of questions and to elicit respondents' trust. A positive rapport was highly salient because some of the questions concerned sensitive topics of inquiry (e.g., sexual behavior) and getting individuals to speak honestly about these topics required first obtaining their trust. Each cultural focus area taps into one or more of the guidelines; a letter code appearing in parentheses specifies which guideline(s) are being probed.

Use of Cyber Environments (A, B, C, E, I, K, L)

- Are you or have you been a member of There.com, IMVU, World of Warcraft or other similar virtual environments in addition to Second Life? How did that work?
- How active are you with texting, Twitter, or instant messaging? Has Second Life changed your involvement with any of these? If so, how?
- What role does Facebook or MySpace have in your life? Has that changed with your involvement in Second Life?
- How do these platforms compare to Second Life? In what ways?
- Do people you don't know sometimes try to add you on Facebook or MySpace? Do you accept them as friends?
- Have you met friends on Facebook or MySpace who then became friends in real life?
- Are all of your friends on Facebook in the United States?
- Do you have Facebook or MySpace friends that you don't know personally? How does that work?
- Do you feel comfortable sharing personal info on Facebook and MySpace?

- Do you try to censor the info you put in your profile, including things like updates or photos?
- What do you think your boss would think of your profile? Would you want them to see it? If you knew it was going to be seen, what would you change?
- How much time do you spend in Second Life compared to other social networking sites or role-playing games like World of Warcraft?

Organizations and Group Involvement (A, B, C, E, J, L)

- What kinds of groups or organizations are you a member of in real life?
- How about Second Life? What groups or organizations are you a part of in Second Life?
- Are you active in groups in Second Life that you are involved with in real life? How does that work?
- How do you parse out your time in Second Life when it comes to balancing your "private" time versus your involvement in organizations?
- Do you find the Second Life limit of 25 group memberships to be limiting? How so?
- What kinds of organizations or groups exist in real life that you wished existed in Second Life? How about the inverse?
- Do you find that group involvement impacts your real-life responsibilities? How so?
- How does your involvement in groups or organizations in Second Life impact your friendships/relationships in either Second Life or real life?

Cultural Identity and Influence (A, B, C, D, E, K, L)

- Do you see yourself as having a cultural or national identity in Second Life? If so, what is it?
- What about your cultural/national identity in real life? How do you recognize it?
- In what ways do you identify yourself? Based upon your religion/country/gender, etc?

- Does being an American impact your involvement in Second Life? Why or why not?
- Have you ever felt that you were either disadvantaged or advantaged by being an American in Second Life? Does it even come up?
- Have you developed relationships with people from foreign countries through Second Life?
- Do you feel more culturally akin to other countries since you joined Second Life?
- How do you see real life culture/nationality manifesting itself in Second Life?
- Have you explored other real-life cultures in Second Life? In what ways did this impact you?
- Have you overlapped with people from other countries in Second Life? How so?
- Has Second Life allowed you to deepen your understanding of other cultures?
- Have you become more sympathetic to other nations since you joined Second Life?
- Do you partake in role-playing areas? Does culture play a part in role-play?
- Do you see role-play involvement as being distinct from your identity/activities when you are not role-playing?
- What part do alts play when it comes to cultural identity? Do you find one alt having a greater concern for cultural loyalties over another alt? Why or why not?

Time Management (E, I)

- How many hours a day/week do you spend in Second Life?
- How does this compare to when you first started with Second Life?
- Does your time in-world fluctuate from one day/week/month to the next?
- Have you ever taken a "break" from Second Life? Tell me about that.
- What's the longest time you've ever spent in-world at one time? What reasons were there for this?
- Describe a time when you have gone in-world for "a few minutes" only to find that hours had gone by?

- Have you ever missed meals, chores, social engagements, or meetings because of Second Life?
- Has Second Life taken precedence over real-life meetings or engagements?
- Have you ever put off things like taking showers or eating meals because of Second Life?
- Have you ever felt compelled to log on to Second Life?
- Have you ever thought or daydreamed about Second Life when at work or doing another activity?
- Has your real-life partner or close friends ever scolded you for spending too much time in Second Life?

Financial Influences (E, F, K, L)

- How much real-life money do you spend in Second Life a week? How about in the total time you've spent in Second Life?
- Have you ever been surprised at the amount of money you spend in Second Life? In what ways is spending money in Second Life different than real life?
- In what ways have you made money in Second Life?
- How does your money-making in Second Life overlap your real-life money management?
- Has your real-life partner ever scolded you for spending too much money on Second Life?
- Have you ever had a job in Second Life? Doing what? How long did you have the job?
- Have you ever made money in Second Life doing things that you'd never do in real life?

Work Impacts (E, I, K, L)

- Has Second Life ever made you late for work, or deprived you of sleep?
- Do you ever think about Second Life at work? How often?
- Have you ever tried accessing Second Life at work?
- Have you ever accessed Second Life instant messenger while at work?

- Have you ever checked to see if your Second Life friends are online while at work?
- Tell me about a time when Second Life affected your real-life job in some way?
- Do you ever talk about Second Life at work?
- Do you ever tell your Second Life friends about work? Give me some examples of what kind of stuff you tell them.
- What do you think your boss would think of your Second Life involvement?
- Would you feel comfortable telling your coworkers about your Second Life avatar and describing the things you do in Second Life?
- Do you know coworkers who are also in Second Life? Do you socialize with them in Second Life?
- Has your involvement in Second Life ever impacted your job performance?

Personal Relationships and Life Impacts (A, B, C, D, E, F, I, K, L)

- Talk about how Second Life impacts your relationships with your real-life partner(s). How about your friends?
- Do you tell your partner about how you spend your time in Second Life? Why or why not?
- Do you feel as though you can open up to your Second Life friends more than you can to your real-life friends?
- Do your friends and family know about your involvement in Second Life? Do they know the extent and the types of activities? What are your thoughts about them knowing?
- Do you or does society consider the activities that take place in Second Life to be taboo or embarrassing? How about things you personally do?
- In what ways does Second Life impact your parenting if you have children, or vice versa?
- What do you think about someone in real life finding out about your Second Life involvement?
- Has anyone ridiculed you for your involvement in Second Life? What happened?
- Do you know people in Second Life that you also know in real life?

- Have you ever recruited anyone else to join Second Life?
- How has your involvement in Second Life affected your real life?
- Do you view Second Life as a way to meet a potential real-life partner?

Behavior Changes and Influences (B, D, E, I, K, L)

- Do you express behaviors in Second Life that you would never express in real life? Can you describe in general?
- How do you think your emotional safety differs in Second Life vs. real life?
- How secure do you feel in Second Life? How about compared to real life? Are there ways you feel less secure in Second Life than real life?
- Have you ever told someone something in Second Life that you would never say in real life?
- Have you ever had anyone influence you to do things in Second Life that you would never do in real life?
- How do your emotional relationships in Second Life impact your real-life emotions?
- Have you ever felt sad in connection to something that happened in Second Life? Tell me about it.
- Have you ever "tracked" the online activities of another avie? Tell me about this.
- What role do alts play in your relationships in Second Life? Describe.
- Have you ever felt guilt picking Second Life over real life? How about the reverse?
- Have you ever used a real-life service through Second Life, such as law advice, website design, education, business meetings, etc?
- Have you ever sought out counseling in Second Life? Do you belong to support groups? Which ones?

Psychological Conditions (E, I)

- Do you use Second Life regularly?
- Do you feel that your personal relationships have suffered as a result of excessive Second Life use?
- Do you conceal your Second Life use from others?

- Do you feel preoccupied by Second Life when offline?
- Do you find it difficult to stay away from Second Life for several days at a time?
- Do you visit Second Life to escape problems or relieve a negative mood?
- Have you tried to cut back on Second Life use? If yes, did you succeed?
- Are you sometimes in Second Life longer than intended? How often?

Misuse of Information Technology (A, B, C, E, F, J, K, L)

- Have you ever partaken in griefing or other self-policing activities in Second Life, or have known anyone who has? What happened?
- Do you know of any instances of using Second Life for illegal activities such as sexual crimes, prostitution, money laundering, or gang/terrorist recruiting?
- What kinds of manipulation do you know of to alter the Second Life software, or manipulate operating system code for personal use?
- Do you know if someone has figured out a way of making a restricted life viewer or bondage implements nonconsensual?
- Have you heard or read about people hacking into the accounts of other residents? For what purpose?
- Have you heard or been impacted by any illegal uses of or in Second Life?
- Do you think there are things that happen in Second Life that should be illegal?
- What do you think about Linden Lab's rule enforcement policies or powers?
- Have you ever experienced or heard of harassment of other residents for deceit or profit?

Appendix D: Real-World Interviews Field Guide

The field guide questions below were used to direct the course of real-world interviews with 10 Second Life residents. Their content is organized around specific topical areas that emerged during group discussions and voice interviews. These topics focus on various domains of personal functioning (e.g., early childhood, daily activities, work life, family life, health issues, etc.) and are distinct from the topics covered during the early phases of data collection. The researchers' primary objective was to understand how respondents came to engage in potentially risky in-world behaviors and what impact these behaviors had on various aspects of their life.

The format of the interviews was semistructured and all questions were worded in an open-ended manner. The researchers, however, tailored the field guide to each respondent, by focusing on areas that were most salient to his or her unique situation, For example, if one respondent practiced a high level of illegal computer activity in-world, researchers focused on learning more about the reasons behind his illegal activities, his childhood and adolescent history with computers, his use of computers in the workplace, etc. If another respondent was favoring his Second Life romantic partnerships in lieu of his own marriage, he was asked numerous follow-up questions about this area of concern. The open-ended, tailored format of questioning resulted in a wealth of information about the respondents. In some cases, however, this information was inconsistent with earlier answers provided during voice interviews and group discussions. These discrepancies are highlighted in the individual case studies for each respondent.

Day-to-Day Activities

- What does a typical weekday look like to you? How about a typical weekend day?
- Tell me what you do in a typical day from the time you get up to the time you go to sleep. Try to be specific about the times that you generally do things.
- Do you take any medications? What are they for?
- What do you think of television? What role does it play in your life?
- How about books? Do you prefer fiction or non-fiction? What was the last book you read?

Work Life

- Describe what it takes to do your job well. What skills do you think you bring to your job that make you stand out from other people?
- What kind of training did you undergo to get your job?

- Tell me about your boss. What is he/she like? How does he/she treat you? What would you want to change about how you're treated?
- What do you think of your coworkers/people you work for?

Evolution of Computer Use

- What were your first experiences with the Internet?
- In what other ways do you use the Internet besides Second Life involvement?
- Describe the other communication avenues the Internet provides for you.
- Describe the "evolution" of your Internet use when it comes to things like blogging, instant messaging, games, and other platforms. What came first? Did one interest evolve into another?

Life and Family

- Tell me about your education.
- Describe your childhood. What was it like?
- Tell me about some of your past jobs.
- Have you ever been in the military? In what capacity?
- How about your family? Do you get along with them?
- Compare your Second Life family to your real-life family.
- What was your real-life social life like before Second Life? Describe it now.
- What is your relationship with your children like?

Relationships

- Describe Second Life relationships that you've had.
- Describe your current marriage/relationship in real life and Second Life.
- In what ways does Second Life enhance your sex life?
- What have your past relationships been like?
- Describe who your avatar is and what it represents to you.

Entry into Second Life

- How did you discover Second Life?
- What about it interested you?
- What was your first experience as a newbie? Did anyone "show you the ropes" or did you feel it out on your own?
- Did you know what you were interested in finding when you first entered Second Life or did others show you things they liked?
- What did you think of Second Life when you first joined? Did it "hook" you immediately or did it take you a while to warm up to it?
- Did anyone try to recruit you as a newbie into any specific area or interest in Second Life?
- Do you find yourself ever helping newbies? In what ways?

Integration of Second Life and Real Life

- Tell me about the last time you took a "break" from Second Life. How long was the break? What precipitated the break? What did you do during the break in your real life? What made you decide to return to Second Life? How did rejoining the Second Life community affect you? Did you find being away from Second Life afforded any benefits in real life?
- In what ways does Second Life become part of who you are in real life?
- Would you recommend that someone you cared about become as involved in Second Life as you are now?
- How would you feel if your child/children were in Second Life? How about your husband or wife?
- How would you describe the affects Second Life has had on your real life? What are three benefits? How about three detriments?

Separation of Second Life and Real Life

- In what ways do you ensure that your Second Life and real life remain separate?
- What is your relationship to your anonymity in Second Life? In what ways do you value it? How does it benefit you?

- Describe several ways that Second Life makes it easier or harder for you to connect with people in real life.

Personality

- How would you describe your personality? How would you describe your avatar's personality?
- In what ways do you think your behavior creates obstacles in your life?
- I'm going to give you an index card and I'd like for you to take a few moments to write a sentence or two describing both your personality and your perceptions of yourself. I won't look at it now, so please be as honest as possible.

Personal/Psychological Issues

- Describe a time when you were not in control of a situation and what happened.
- Do you ever have problems getting to sleep at night or staying asleep?
- Are you ever edgy, restless, or have feelings of unease? How does Second Life help/exacerbate these feelings?
- What kinds of things do you worry about in your day-to-day life? How about in Second Life?
- Do you ever feel any physical issues that are bothersome, but that you don't think are big enough a deal to see a doctor about? Things like dizzy spells, neck or backaches, or frequent headaches?
- Tell me what your future will look like.
- Do you ever feel like you have lost confidence in yourself or feel critical of your life?
- Has anyone ever told you that you have to be in control of everything?
- Describe some of your "pet peeves" around your home. What irritates you when it comes to housekeeping issues?
- Describe three things that you just have to have your way? What happens when they change?
- How have you changed as a person since entering Second Life?

Now I'm going to quote what other residents have said about SECOND LIFE and I'd like you to respond to each quote:

- I'm totally ashamed of Second Life.
- Sometimes I have to "make" myself go be real.
- I think having some "me" time in Second Life has made me a better parent. I was too "focused" on being just a mommy before, now that I have a social life in Second Life, so I have a better perspective on my kids' problems.
- I don't trust anyone, but nowadays it isn't keeping me from communicating with people.
- I find it less stressful to talk to people in Second Life, so I've chosen Second Life over real life for social things.
- Second Life helps me tackle some real-life problems better. I can talk to a friend or someone on Second Life that might have went through what I'm going through at the moment.
- This place is kind of sickening to normal people.
- I don't think Second Life changes people, I think, like adversity, Second Life just reveals who they really are and sometimes that is not very pretty.
- You have people trapped in their homes who are often afraid to interact socially because of low or no self esteem and you promise them the moon and all the stars and they never have to bleed at first.
- I schedule to be in Second Life when my partner is here.
- There are always people who want to create drama and make things harder for you. Just like in real life.
- It's very easy for me to lose time in Second Life.
- If you're not part of Second Life you just can't understand.
- It's a trial by error sort of thing, you grant people the right to know things about your Second Life in hopes that they will keep it confidential.
- I think the relative anonymity that Second Life provides encourages people to be more adventurous than they perhaps might be if their real identities were at stake.
- My dream job is where I can spend time in Second Life without getting in trouble for it.
- My Second Life is a big part of my real life. If I need a recipe, I ask a friend. If my friend likes a band, I look them up. Second Life is part of my day-to-day life.

- In Second Life I feel more jealous; chances of cheating are greater, reading the ex's profile, etc.
- I feel I'm a better person in real life because Second Life allowed me to practice healthier behaviors that I was too scared to try out in real life.
- I am better in real life because of Second Life, not in spite of it.

APPENDIX E: LIST OF BEHAVIORAL CATEGORIES

Addiction: Discussions about addiction to Second Life or addiction to substances or activities.

Alts: Discussions of use, benefits, and disadvantages of alternate avatars.

Anonymity: Meaning, use, benefits, and disadvantages of anonymity to residents.

Background: Real-life demographics and lifestyle characteristics of residents.

Blogging: Writing or reading of blogs.

Control: The desire for control in real life or in Second Life.

Creation: Appreciation or creation of art and objects in Second Life.

Criminal Behavior: Descriptions of illegal real-life behaviors.

Emotion: Experience of real-life emotions in Second Life and effect of Second Life on emotional well-being.

Entry into Second Life: Experience of first learning about Second Life and subsequently entering it.

Facebook/My Space: Differences and similarities between Facebook/MySpace and Second Life.

Foreign: Discussions about seeking out and/or meeting foreign residents and issues of nationality and cultural identity.

Groups: Involvement in Second Life groups and opinions regarding their differences from real-life groups.

Honesty: Illustrations of what honesty means in Second Life and stories of honesty/dishonesty encountered in-world.

Identity: Differences and similarities between residents' identity in real life vs. Second Life.

Illegal: Descriptions of illegal activities in Second Life either committed by residents or others they know.

Influence: Stories of avatars influencing others or being influenced by someone else.

Information Technology (IT): Computer knowledge, scripting, coding, and manipulation of others in-world through IT.

Life: Reflections on real-life habits and behaviors.

Money: Discussions about real-life finances and Second Life expenditures.

Neglect of Family: Stories of neglecting family members or family members complaining about neglect.

Neglect of Friends: Stories of neglecting friends or having friends complain about neglect and withdrawal.

Neglect of Work: Stories and examples of when Second Life has negatively affected residents' real-life work.

Pedophilia: Rumors and stories of pedophilia and reflections on child avatars and age-play.

Psychological Concerns: Illustrations of concerning behaviors of psychological nature.

Real Life/Second Life Overlap: Specific stories of the impact of Second Life on real life.

Recruitment: Stories of being recruited as a newbie into specific subcultures of Second Life.

Relationships: Discussions about real-life and Second Life relationships, including similarities and differences between them.

Role-Play: Examples of residents' experience with role-play in Second Life.

Rules: Discussions about Second Life rules, their perceptions, and stories on keeping or breaking the rules.

Sex: Discussions and stories about cyber sex.

Second Life Benefits: Residents' examples of positive benefits of Second Life for their real life.

Second Life Breaks: Accounts of taking a break from Second Life, including why the break occurred and why the individual chose to come back.

Seconds Life Negatives: Resident-identified disadvantages of Second Life for real-life outcomes.

Self-Neglect: Stories about poor self-care and neglect of basic needs and health. **Social Networking**: General discussions about social networking via the Internet.

Substitute: Stories of when and why Second Life becomes a substitute for real-life activities.

Time: Discussions about amount of time spent in Second Life relative to time spent in real-life activities.

Virtual Environments: General discussions about virtual realities and their role in today's world.

Work: Accounts of Second Life's impact on residents' real-life jobs.

End Note

[1] Linden Lab has drawn a great deal of international attention due to age-play, and some countries legally treat simulated pedophilia as real child pornography. In addition, there is evidence that many age-play practitioners have moved to other virtual environments. See Report I for additional detail.

INDEX

C

F

Q

R

S

T

U

V

W

Y